LIFE

ON

PURPOSE

Six Passages to an
Inspired Life

by W. Bradford Swift

www.lifeonpurpose.com

Elite Books

Santa Rosa, CA 95403

www.EliteBooksOnline.com

Library of Congress Cataloging-in-Publication Data

Swift, W. Bradford

Life on purpose : six passages to an inspired life / by W. Bradford Swift.— 1st ed.

    p. cm.

ISBN-13: 978-1-60070-023-1 (hardcover)
ISBN-10: 1-60070-023-3 (hardcover)
ISBN-13: 978-1-60070-024-8 (softcover)
ISBN-10: 1-60070-024-1 (softcover)

1. Conduct of life. 2. Intention—Religious aspects. 3. Spiritual life. 4. Life. 5. Personal coaching. I. Title.

BJ1581.2.S924 2007

170'.44—dc22

2007010599

Cover design by Victoria Valentine

Typesetting by Karin Kinsey

Copyedited by Courtney Arnold

Typeset in Cochin

Printed in USA

First Edition

10 9 8 7 6 5 4 3 2 1

This is the true joy in life, the being used for a purpose recognized by yourself as a mighty one, being thoroughly worn out before you are thrown on the scrap heap, the being a force of nature instead of a feverish little clod of ailments and grievances complaining that the world will not devote itself to making you happy.

—George Bernard Shaw

DEDICATION

I dedicate this book to the powerful and purposeful women who have surrounded me as I've traveled along my own Purposeful Path. This includes my mother, Pattie, who, after my father passed away when I was almost seven, also served in many ways as my dad, and who prepared me so well for life's journey. It also includes my coaches: Judy Billman, my first coach, who introduced me so well to the power of a coaching relationship; Jayne Smith and Nancy Dorrier, who coached me during many times of transition; Michele Lisenbury Christensen, who served as my midwife as I gave birth to Life on Purpose Institute in the mid-nineties; and Andrea Lee, whose living example and coaching continues to help me guide Life on Purpose into its second decade.

I also dedicate this book to the purposeful and passionate people who make up the Life on Purpose Community, especially my clients who have allowed me to serve them as their Life Purpose Coach, and in doing so, gave me room to express my own life purpose.

And most of all, I dedicate this book and all my life en-deavors to the two most magnificently beautiful, caring, and compassionate women in my life: my wife, Ann, and my daughter, Amber. I dedicate this book to the two of you. May your journey along your own Purposeful Path always be filled with passion, play, and peace of mind. I love, honor, and cherish you both.

ACKNOWLEDGMENTS

There is a popular saying that it takes a village to raise a child. Well, I have found out that it takes at least a village to write, publish, and promote a book. So, in addition to those I've already acknowledged in my dedication, I'd also like to thank the following people:

The members of the Visionary Writers on Purpose team, who have listened week in and week out as I shared about the slow progress of pulling this book project together, and, most of all, for continuing to be a source of inspiration and support.

Dawson Church and his support team at Elite Books and Author's Publishing, for shepherding me through the process of publishing and marketing this book.

And I give a special thanks to my good friend Eric Miller, whose generosity and steadfast belief in this book project and in me made it all possible.

CONTENTS

A LIFE ON PURPOSE IN A WORLD ON PURPOSE

What would it be like to understand your Divinely Inspired Life Purpose with crystal clarity? Right in this moment, you can begin to experience your life on purpose. Imagine that you know and are deeply in touch with your vision for what's possible, like when you were a child just starting out on this bold adventure called life. Imagine also that you know and are deeply in touch with your core values—those intangibles that mean the most to you—and that you know and are deeply in touch with the essence of who you are. Finally, imagine that all of this is bound together and connected by the attractive power of Universal Love, your relationship with God or a higher power, and by your spiritual nature.

Through this book, it is my interest and intention to create a powerful and purposeful coaching relationship with you, one that is perhaps best summed up by these words from the Life on Purpose Coaches Creed:

Imagine a relationship in which the total focus is on you, on your life purpose, and on living true to it…

Imagine someone listening not only to your words, but also to the soul behind them as it expresses its truest desires…

Imagine someone who will be your partner as you hold yourself accountable for living true to your life purpose…

Imagine that this person is curious about your dreams and aspirations, your vision for the world, and what you are most passionate about in your life. This is a person who will help you clarify projects that are consistent with your vision, your values, and who you are, and will help you develop the means to fulfill them...

Imagine a relationship with a person who may, at times, appear even more committed to what you want in your life than you are...

Imagine that in this relationship you can count on this person to absolutely tell you the truth with ruthless compassion—about the many gifts and talents that perhaps you've taken for granted, as well as where you might be selling out on who you really are...

Imagine a relationship that supports you in breaking free from the self-limiting constraints of your past, in which the voice now exposing your limitations is recognized for what it is—a voice from the past. Imagine that your true spirit is nurtured to shape and form your life, moment by moment, day by day.

Imagine every aspect of your life being shaped by your Divinely Inspired Life Purpose. Your actions are shaped by your life purpose; your thoughts, decisions, choices...all shaped by your life purpose, which comes from the blending of your vision, your values, and the essence of your being together with Universal Love and your spiritual nature.

What would such a life be like? Imagine it right now, for just a moment or two.

What would you experience, living such a life? What would it feel like to know your life purpose so clearly that it would have the power to shape each moment and all that you do?

What would your life look like? What are some of the things you'd be doing as true expressions of your vision, your values, and the essence of your soul? What would you no longer do because it would be inconsistent with your life purpose? Imagine the magical nature of such a life.

What would be different about your life? And what would likely be the same? What would you have in your life, and what would you no longer have—simply because it is inconsistent with your life purpose?

Now, let's stretch our imagination just a bit more. Imagine that you're living in a world where everyone knows his or her life purpose and is living true to it. In other words, you're living on purpose in a World on Purpose. Can you imagine such a life? What would that be like?

This book outlines the Life on Purpose Process—a proven, systematic, spiritually based, and practical approach that has already assisted thousands of people to clarify their Divinely Inspired Life Purpose and to begin to live a life beyond what they could have initially imagined. Are you ready to begin your journey along the Purposeful Path to such a life? If so, here's your first coaching assignment:

After pondering about the questions above, write down your thoughts about each one and share them with someone whom you care deeply about. Explore this world on purpose with him or her.

MY PERSONAL JOURNEY
ALONG THE PURPOSEFUL PATH

As part of my early morning spiritual practices, I often trudge up the footpaths that wind around Glassy Mountain behind Carl Sandburg's home, a few blocks from my home in Flat Rock, North Carolina. On this morning, as I stop to catch my breath, my mind flashes to an ugly yet necessary time in the early 1980s. I'm on the bathroom floor in my apartment in Greensboro during another period of contemplation. Sobbing and in a fetal position, I can't remember how I ended up here or how long I've been this way. I know only that I'm in great emotional pain and will do anything to make it stop. I imagine what I might do if I had a gun. Would I have the nerve to use it? If I did, would I screw it up like I'd screwed up the rest of my life? The more I think about it, the more real the gun becomes, until finally I realize it's not my imagination but a real gun—which I hold in my hand.

I feel the smooth wooden handle in my palm and the cold metal circle of the snub nose pressed against my temple. My finger begins to tighten on the trigger. Just a little more pressure, a quick flash of pain, and the deeper pain will finally be over. Funny, I think as I lay there, how many people will be surprised to learn of my suicide. To outward appearances, I've got it made: my own veterinary practice, investments in real estate, a fancy car, a wallet full of credit cards—all the trimmings of a supposedly successful life. But beneath the well-crafted exterior is a hollow core of emptiness and suffering. My life feels worthless, without any real meaning. All the adornments of my Good Life don't add up to true happiness or fulfillment. The truth is I feel alone in the world, with no one who truly cares about me or understands what I'm going through.

Suddenly, someone has invaded my privacy. "Go away," I think as loudly as I can, then realize I'm also shouting it. "Go away! Leave me alone!"

But whoever it is doesn't leave. A moment later I smell the pleasant fragrance of a woman's perfume, then hear the voice of an angel. "It's okay, Brad. We're going to get you some help. It's okay." I recognize the voice of my friend Rebecca.

Now, as I sit watching the exquisite sunrise over the Blue Ridge Mountains, that day in Greensboro seems to be from a different person's life—and in many ways it is. I am no longer that confused, scared, lonely young man. I no longer practice veterinary medicine; instead, I'm the founder of the spiritually based Life on Purpose Institute. And today I can truthfully say my life is filled with purpose and meaning.

The journey of the last two decades has been a wild roller coaster ride filled with slow upward climbs and exciting, sometimes scary descents. It is what I affectionately term my Purposeful Path. Before my near-suicide I traveled the path mostly asleep, unaware that I was even on a journey. Then came ten years of awakening, with a few long naps mixed in. And for the last decade, as I've continued my awakening process, I've done my best to assist others along their own Purposeful Path. What follows are some of the key stops along the way.

Chasing the Red Queen

I'd like to say that after my near-suicide my life was suddenly and miraculously transformed…but my mother told me to never lie. The truth is that my transformation was slow and arduous—a journey of many trials and errors, with a number of side trips and more than a few dead ends.

My next significant moment of awakening came a few years later, during my second marriage. At that time, I was still caught up in the great American Dream of acquiring as many expensive toys as possible and had a lovely companion who was just as good at the acquisition game. We lived in a plush neighborhood, on an acre of land, in a beautiful home complete with a rear deck overlooking a babbling brook.

Unfortunately, I was working too much to enjoy any of it. I felt like Alice in Wonderland. In Lewis Carroll's childhood classic *Through the Looking-Glass*, one of Alice's misadventures in Wonderland is with the Red Queen, who takes her on a wild run through the countryside. But no matter how fast Alice runs she can't seem to get anywhere. Finally, breathless from her efforts, Alice is allowed to rest long enough to comment, "Everything is just as it was!" The Queen replies, "Here, you see, it takes all the running you can do, to keep in the same place. If you want to get somewhere else, you must run at least twice as fast as that!"

I knew just how Alice must have felt. I was physically exhausted and emotionally out of breath, running as fast as I could to keep up with an out-of-control lifestyle of my own making. As I gazed across the wooded lot and listened to the bubbling of the water across the rocks, I realized that much of my reason for purchasing the home had been that very scene. At the time I had imagined spending countless hours out on the deck, basking in the sun, watching the seasons roll by—but the seasons had rolled by without me. I'd not so much as stepped foot on the deck in all that time. I'd been too busy working fifty to sixty hours a week at my veterinary practice so that I could pay the mortgage on the house and keep two car payments up and three credit cards paid down. Like Alice, I realized something was wrong with this picture. I was running as fast as I could just to keep up.

While I still hadn't suffered quite enough to make any radical changes, a seed of "divine discontent" had been planted. Unfortunately, it wasn't until my second marriage ended in divorce and I came close to professional burnout that the lesson finally hit home.

The Complexities of Simple Living

My personal journey to a simpler, more purposeful life was motivated by two factors: fatigue and frustration. I'd been on the fast track ever since taking my first part-time job at the age of fifteen, working at the library downtown. I held my nose to the proverbial grind stone through junior and senior high school, being sure to make the types of grades that would prove to the world that I was worthy of attending veterinary college. I even managed to rush through undergraduate school, completing a four-year pre-vet program in less than three. By the time the mid-1980s rolled around, I had been hoofing it hot and heavy for over twenty years and, by American standards, I was a success. Yet, despite all the trappings of success, I kept thinking, "Is this all there is?"

My frustration grew out of a lack of meaningful ways to express my natural creative interests. Although my art teachers in high school had urged me to continue studying art in college, I would hear none of it. I knew that artists starved and veterinarians didn't. Yet, by the time I found myself standing on my deck contemplating the similarities between Alice's predicament and my own, I was starved—creatively and spiritually.

Awakening to a Purposeful Life of Service

After over twelve years of struggling in private practice, I finally decided to seek help to grow my business. During an initial interview, Judy Billman, a business consultant whom one of my colleagues had recommended, asked me a question that no one— not even I—had ever asked.

"Dr. Swift, do you want to continue to be a veterinarian?"

My eyes teared up with the realization that the answer was, "No." But if I left practice at that point, I would feel as if I'd failed.

"I want to go out the top not the back door," I told Judy, and hired her to help me accomplish that feat. Fortunately for me, Judy turned out to be more than a business consultant. She was my first exposure to coaching. Rather than spending most of the time looking over my financial records or my inventory, I spent it looking within myself. What I discovered was that while I was comfortable with my four-footed patients, I was terrified of their two-legged companions at the other end of the leash. And my reluctance to be with my clients was stifling my practice.

In the process of working with Judy I also rediscovered my true reason for entering the veterinary profession in the first place, which was to serve and make a difference both with people and their pets. Somewhere in the midst of the long hours spent struggling to make ends meet, I'd lost touch with this deeper purpose. My practice had never grown by more than 15% in any other year; but upon reawakening to this deeper sense of purpose, it grew by over 40% in the first year that I worked with Judy. Most importantly, in the process, I fell back in love with practice. This created a bit of a dilemma. After all, I'd hired Judy to help build the practice so I could sell it. I'd also found a new outlet for my creativity in writing and was having some early success selling magazine articles. Yet, suddenly, here I was having the best time of my professional life.

For the first time ever I experienced true choice: I realized that, whether I kept the practice or sold it, I could be happy as long as I was making a difference and being of service. Though still a fairly vague life purpose, it was enough to begin to shape my life and decisions. Realizing that I had now accomplished what I had set out to do as a veterinarian, I sold my practice to pursue my dream of being a writer. And recognizing the profound difference coaching had made in my life, I also added the dream of becoming a coach. A year after selling my veterinary practice, I joined the coaching and consulting firm where Judy now worked and where I learned further skills as a business coach.

The Transformational Power of Purpose

My next significant moment of awakening came during a spiritual retreat in Mentone, Alabama. We were learning about the spiritual laws of prosperity, specifically the idea that we all have a divine life purpose, when I realized at least a part of my own life purpose was to assist others in identifying and living true to theirs. I had stopped business coaching about a year before to concentrate on my writing, but continued developing my skills as a life coach by volunteering for a personal development company.

A few months later, in an effort to bring more purpose to my free-lance writing, I created Project Purpose. The goal of the project was to write and publish articles about people and institutions whose lives and missions were dedicated to a bold and inspired purpose or vision. Up to that point, most other writers and editors knew me as a former small animal veterinarian who could write a clear and publishable article about pets, animals, or health-related issues. But even though I'd only written one or two profiles in over six years of freelance writing, I was excited to see whether I could redirect my writing career by following the passion I found in exploring my life purpose.

A couple months after creating Project Purpose, while attending the second spiritual retreat of my life, I met Bo Lozoff, co-founder of the Human Kindness Foundation.[1] After listening to his two keynote talks I knew that this quietly powerful man had a message many more people needed to hear. I introduced myself and informed Bo that I planned to write an article about his work of reawakening the spiritual nature of prisoners through his Prison-Ashram Project. At the time, I didn't have a clue what magazine would take such an article. Surely none of the editors of the pet and health publications I was accustomed to writing for would be interested.

Still, I followed this new passion for purpose by sending a barrage of query letters about Bo to every magazine I could imagine that might be interested in sharing the wisdom of this modern day sage with their readers. A few weeks later I received a call from Jon Adolph, then editor-in-chief of *New Age Journal,* asking me to write a feature article for their publication — even though I'd never written for them before. Of course, I jumped at the chance.

---

1 www.humankindness.org.

It was one of the most satisfying writing experiences of my life. I loved conducting the research, including a visit to the Human Kindness Foundation not far from my home and an "impossible" telephone interview with a prison inmate in one of this country's highest security prisons. Writing the article was exhilarating and even the revision process was nearly painless. When I received a check for more than double what I had previously received for any one article, I knew I was onto something big. That first assignment was just the beginning. I continued to follow the breadcrumbs of my purpose and passion, and began realizing my intention of inspiring other people to live more purposeful lives as well. What I didn't expect was that one of the people most inspired by the articles would be me.

I conducted dozens of interviews with incredible people, and I noticed that many of them were expressing their life purpose through service to others in some structured, organized way. It finally dawned on me that if they could do it, so could I. Thus, the seed of a new enterprise was planted; but it would take another Project Purpose article to germinate it.

The Birth of Life on Purpose

The article that gave birth to my own purpose-inspired enterprise was an assignment, entitled "Simple Living in a Complex World," for *Yoga Journal.* Since Ann and I had been actively involved with the voluntary simplicity movement for years, this was a perfect writing assignment for me. When they asked me to also write a resource sidebar, I decided to include Life on Purpose, the name of the organization I wanted to launch. After all, the tagline for my dream organization was "A Life on Purpose is a life of service, simplicity, and spiritual serenity."

I still remember the day, a few weeks after the article appeared as the cover story for *Yoga Journal,* when the phone rang. Pausing from my work, I answered in my accustomed way: "Hello, this is Brad."

"Is this Life on Purpose?" an enthusiastic voice asked on the other end of the line.

I paused, momentarily confused, and looked around my office. Well, yes, I guess it was. "Yes, this is Life on Purpose. How may I be of service?" I replied with only a moment of hesitation.

The gentleman, a psychologist in California, had just read the *Yoga Journal* piece and really resonated with the message, especially the idea of living a life of service, simplicity, and spiritual serenity. "Could you send me some information about your organization?" he asked.

Again, with even less hesitation, I took a deep gulp and replied, "Sure. I'll send something to you in just a few days." Of course, I didn't have any material at that time—not even a business card or brochure. But I did have a lot of ideas and pages and pages of notes in my computer. I spent the next few days creating materials to send to him. In the process, Life on Purpose Institute was born.

Creating a World on Purpose

One of my goals in founding Life on Purpose Institute was to bring together two things I love and am most passionate about: coaching and life purpose. This became Life Purpose Coaching. It didn't make sense to me that so many people had to take thirty, forty, or more years of their lives to finally clarify their life purpose. Was it really necessary for it to take so long? Couldn't we somehow shorten the learning curve just a bit so we could get on with living our purpose?

As I asked these questions, answers came from my inner guidance. It didn't take long for these answers to coalesce into a systematic, spiritually based process for assisting people to clarify and live true to their life purpose. It also became the model for my Life Purpose Coaching.

But how could I make this process available to people? Would it even work? Where would I find people to try it out on? Again, I asked these questions of my inner guidance and received answers.

While working for the coaching and consulting company, one of my primary jobs had been creating new business through cold-calling companies. While I became fairly good at it, I never enjoyed it. In fact, it was one of the reasons I eventually left the company.

So, I made a pact with God. "I'll do whatever it takes to bring this dream into reality," I prayed to God, "except cold calls. We'll have to find another way."

Once again I followed my passion to find the answer. I'd always been fascinated by the Internet, as well as having been an avid CompuServe fan even before the popularity of the World Wide Web. So, I created my own homemade web site. Much to my surprise, it began to attract my first coaching clients for what I had named the Life on Purpose Process.

And the Life on Purpose Process worked. In fact, it worked extremely well—beyond anything I had imagined. My clients were transforming their lives, and rather than taking years of trial and error to clarify their life purpose, they were becoming crystal clear in a matter of weeks. Clearly, the Life on Purpose Process was divinely inspired.

For example, one of my first clients to be guided through the Life on Purpose Process had been a struggling small business owner. As he clarified his true purpose, he realized that he longed to live in a more exotic location and to bring a deeper sense of adventure to his life, while continuing to utilize his talents as a "people person." Here's what he experienced as a result of traveling along the Purposeful Path, using the Life on Purpose Process as his roadmap and me as his guide and coach:

When I first started I felt as though I was swimming upstream, struggling to keep my business afloat. While I enjoyed the artistic satisfaction of the video production business, I realized I was mainly working just to provide an income for my family. As I worked through the Life on Purpose Process, I began to believe that I could actually choose where I wanted to live and what I wanted to do.

After fourteen years in the video business, I had to gamble that moving four hours away and working in a completely different industry was worth the risk. I banked on the adventurous part of me, which I'd identified was part of my true purpose, and gave it a try.

Moving to Myrtle Beach was one of the best moves of my life. My family loves it here, and I feel fortunate to be able to run on the beach two or three times a week every week. I am proud to be working at one of the finest gated oceanfront resort communities on the East Coast. I interact with some of the most interesting and successful people I could ever have the chance to meet, and that has influenced me in such positive ways. So this new job is more aligned with my true life purpose.

I learned from the Life on Purpose Process that much of my life had been shaped by fear that lead me to believe that I have to work, work, work, and can't have fun. These beliefs kept me in a job for fourteen years with no sight of increased pay or satisfaction. Stepping out of that daily grind was the impetus to a life I dreamed about.

–Eric Miller

With my clients reporting such results, I soon realized that the subject of life purpose had universal appeal. I had a tiger by the tail. As my homemade web site began to attract interest from around the world, I began to wonder what would happen if I had a professionally designed web site. The answer was that even more people were attracted to Life on Purpose Institute. It wasn't long before my own life of service, simplicity, and spiritual serenity was in jeopardy—especially the simplicity and serenity parts. How could I fulfill the world's deep hunger for purpose and still keep my own life in balance? It finally dawned on me that I needed to replicate my efforts; so, in 1999, I created the Coaches Development Program to train Life Purpose Coaches.

And I've never looked back! Since that auspicious birth, Life on Purpose Institute has gone on to help thousands of people to clarify and live true to their life purpose. As the founder and Chief Visionary Officer, my days are filled with purpose, passion, and play. I still don't know where my purpose will ultimately take me, but I plan to enjoy the journey every step of the way. After all, a Life on Purpose is meant to be lived lifelong.

But Enough About Me

I love to share the story of my journey along the Purposeful Path, but this book is really intended as a personal guidebook to assist you.

First, you'll uncover what's been standing in your way and move it aside, opening yourself to do the inner work of clarifying your true, Divinely Inspired Life Purpose. At that point, the real fun and adventure begins as you step onto the lifelong path of living true to the life purpose that has revealed itself.

So, let's start by becoming clear about why it's so important to begin this journey in the first place...

WHY BEGIN THE JOURNEY?

What is a life purpose? At first glance it may seem like the answer to this question is so obvious that it's pointless to even discuss it. But I have found that there is often a wealth of wisdom in questions we assume we already know how to answer.

I've dedicated my life to exploring many of the different facets and nuances of the idea of life purpose. In 1996 I founded Life on Purpose Institute as a way to explore questions like, "What is a life purpose?" Consequently, I've had the privilege to ask thousands of people that question and many others. I've discovered some very interesting things about our relationship to the notion of having a life purpose. And in one sense, you could say that this book is all about what I've discovered in the process.

For example, I've discovered that most people answer the question, "What is a life purpose," in a very similar way. Oh, they may use some different words, but the core theme of their responses is quite similar. In other words, there's a common cultural response to the question. Unfortunately, this cultural response has acted as an undetected detour sign, diverting most people off the Purposeful Path right from the start. As a result, when many people ask the more personal question, "What is *my* life purpose?" the answers they come up with are already off the mark.

This book is about exploring a different response to the question, "What is a life purpose?" I have found that looking at this question from a different angle, also known as the Life on Purpose Perspective, opens a whole new and different, purposeful pathway to explore and leads people to a place on the map that was previously hidden from view. I consider it to be the birthplace of people's true, Divinely Inspired Life Purpose. But let's not get ahead of ourselves. Let's first answer the question, "Why is it important to bring clarity of purpose to our lives?"

Check the News

Pick up any major newspaper or spend half an hour viewing the evening news. Looks pretty bad, doesn't it? We're killing each other in unprecedented numbers and we're killing the Earth. Here are some alarming facts:

- According to the Federal Bureau of Investigation, there were over 16,000 cases of homicide in the United States in 2004

- According to the same source, over 94,000 cases of forcible rape occurred in the same year.

- In 2004, over 850,000 cases of aggravated assault were reported.

- According to Dr. Richard Leakey, the world's most famous paleoanthropologist, between 17,000 and 100,000 species vanish from our planet each year. "For the sake of argument, let's assume the number is 50,000 a year. Whatever way you look at it, we're destroying the Earth at a rate comparable with the impact of a giant asteroid slamming into the planet, or even a shower of vast heavenly bodies."[2]

- Americans go to the mall more frequently than we go to church or engage in some other form of spiritual practice. Over 90% of teenage girls in the U. S. consider shopping their favorite pastime, and most teens spend as much time at the mall as at their homes and schools combined.[3]

2 *The Sixth Extinction* by Richard Leakey and Roger Lewin (Doubleday, 1995).
3 *E Magazine*, April 1996.

Many people say we're going to hell in a hand basket, that it's too late for us. They say these facts prove we are inherently evil and that we're doomed to perish. Others blame our government. The rich and affluent point to the poor and unemployed as the problem, while the poor and middle-class say it's our economic system. The rich get richer while the poor…well, you know the line.

But I don't see it this way. I see another possibility. When I look at what's happening, I see a world without vision and people without purpose. There's nothing wrong, only something missing. As it says in the Bible, "Without vision, the people perish." This is true for all people, not just Christians. When we don't know why we're truly here, we tend to get into a lot of mischief—much of which is destructive to ourselves and to the world. Just check the news.

Settle back in your chair for a moment, set aside your cynicism, and take a couple of deep, relaxing breaths. See yourself reading a newspaper in which the headlines reflect a world where all people truly know why they are here on planet Earth. Not only do they know their purpose in life, but they are living true to it consistently. Can you imagine what life would be like in such a world? Can you allow even a glimmer of this possibility to shine through? Imagine reading headlines like these:

- Lasting Peace Achieved in the Middle East
- World Leaders Declare the End of Hunger in this Decade
- Largest Number of Interfaith Leaders Gather in Jerusalem

That's what this book is about, clear and simple. It's about transforming the world from one that's off purpose to one on purpose—one person at a time.

Will you be one of those people?

I believe in a world where there are no accidents. It wasn't a mistake or an accident that you picked up this book. Of course, I'm not so idealistic as to think that a book is all you need to transform your life. But I do believe it can be the catalyst that starts the process, or that takes the process to the next level. I've seen it countless times before in my own life and in the lives of hundreds, if not thousands, of other people—many of whom I've worked with as their Life Purpose Coach.

THE SIX PASSAGES
OF THE PURPOSEFUL PATH

1. Preparing for the Journey Along the Purposeful Path

As with any challenging journey, it's best to thoroughly prepare yourself for your travels along the Purposeful Path. This includes accurately determining where you are starting from and where you intend to end up, as well as knowing some of the obstacles that could possibly get in the way of completing the journey. Purposeful Preparation is important to a successful journey. The title of David Campbell's book sums it up well: *If You Don't Know Where You're Going, You'll Probably End up Somewhere Else.*

2. Starting on the Purposeful Path with the Life on Purpose Perspective

Of course, it makes sense to begin your journey on the path that will get you where you want to go most expediently. We'll explore how most people have thought of a life purpose, which we call the Cultural Perspective, and how this can be a major detour away from your true purpose. We'll then look in depth at the Life on Purpose Perspective that opens a door to a new world of purpose and possibility.

3. Uncovering What Has Been Shaping Your Life: Your Inherited Purpose

Another key passage along the Purposeful Path is clearly identifying what has been shaping your life and keeping you from clarifying and living your true, Divinely Inspired Life Purpose. We call this the Inherited Purpose—a powerful force based in fear, lack, and a need to struggle to survive that shapes our lives much of the time, especially when we're unclear about our true purpose. Many who have already traveled along the Purposeful Path feel that identifying their specific and unique Inherited Purpose is one of the most powerful, transforming parts of the process.

4. **Clarifying and Polishing Your True, Divinely Inspired Purpose**

After cleaning the slate by identifying and beginning to be responsible for your Inherited Purpose, the real fun begins as you go through a process called Priming Your Passion to clarify your true, Divinely Inspired life purpose. The process can be not only life affirming, but also life transforming. This completes Stage One, or the clarifying your life purpose stage.

5. **Learning the Tools for Living on Purpose**

This is the start of Stage Two of the process, in which you begin to live true to your life purpose. It is where the rubber meets the road, and where some of the biggest transformations take place as you're introduced to Sixteen Power Tools for Living on Purpose. You will use these tools to begin to build your Life on Purpose.

6. **Mastering the Tools for Living on Purpose**

Of course, being introduced to a set of tools is just the beginning—especially if you're interested in building a masterpiece of a Life on Purpose. In this next part you will learn how to master the art and science of creating a life that is shaped by your true, Divinely Inspired Life Purpose.

The Roller Coaster Ride of Transformation

The Life on Purpose Process is a transformational process, and sometimes transformation can be uncomfortable. The deeper you let yourself go, the more transformed you will be when you come out the other side. This process is much like a roller coaster ride. Some people love roller coasters, while others hate them. The same is true about going through the Life on Purpose Process.

Here is a partial list of ways to experience this ride:

- Excited and thrilled
- Scared and fearful
- Frustrated and angry (i.e., committed to not enjoying or benefiting from the process)
- Bored and indifferent

I encourage you to be committed to the whole ride. In other words, don't get off while the car is in motion or until you've completed the whole process—including and especially the assignments! Also, commit to the fact that those around you also benefit from your taking the ride.

If you honor this request and these commitments, you will dramatically increase the value you and those around you will receive from the process of clarifying your life purpose.

All Aboard!

MEET THE BOOMERS

Meet Bob and Barbara Boomer. Bob is closing in on sixty, while Barbara is in her mid-fifties. They've been married, more or less happily, for over twenty-five years. They have three children: Becky, twenty-four, who recently graduated from college and is searching for the career that will make her happy; Brent, twenty-two, who is in his junior year of college; and Brandon, seventeen, who will be graduating from high school this year and will likely go on to college—although he hasn't a clue which one or what he wants to study.

The Boomers are a typical family, and being American, their lives have been shaped by the pursuit of the Great American Dream. Until recently, neither Bob nor Barbara has given much thought to the idea of having a life purpose. If you were to corner them into talking about it, though, their views would be consistent with the common Cultural Perspective that a life purpose is what one is to do while alive on Earth. But recently, one of Barbara's friends gave her a book that started her thinking more about her purpose in life, and which then led to her sharing her thoughts with another good friend—her husband, Bob.

Because he thought of life purpose as "what I'm here to do," when Bob went to find purpose and meaning for his own life, he went the route of work. On the strong advisement of his parents, he became a dentist like his dad. He graduated from dental school with honors and worked for five years as an associate before opening his own practice, which he has had for over twenty years. While he won't admit it to anyone but Barbara, he's pretty burned out from having looked into thousands of mouths for over two decades, and the sense of purpose in his work has dried up. Still, since he has college tuitions to cover, a hefty mortgage on their 2,500-sqare-foot home, and monthly bills to pay, "off to work I go" has become Bob's theme song.

The upside of Bob's focusing so heavily on work is that he has become a very successful dentist and a prominent member of his community. The downside is that, in the process, the rest of his life has been thrown out of balance in the following ways:

- He's alienated from his wife and children.

- He has no real time for friends, only professional colleagues.

- He doesn't really have any hobbies or interests outside work.

- Spiritual life…what's that? He hasn't gone to church since his wedding to Barbara and while he does believe in God, he hasn't bothered to be in touch since he was a child. Late at night, however, when he can't sleep (which is often), he wonders if there isn't more to life than he's experiencing. He suspects the answer is a resounding "Yes."

- His health is poor by most people's standards, though fairly typical for those in his profession. He's about twenty pounds overweight, has high blood pressure and insomnia, and is addicted to watching late night TV as a way to de-stress from his work.

Barbara, on the other hand, considers it her purpose in life to be a good mother and a supportive wife to Bob. One of her greatest worries is what she'll do with herself once Brandon leaves home—which is due to happen in less than a year. It was because of this that her friend recommended *Life on Purpose.* She also finds herself awake at night asking herself such questions as "Who am I? Am I really just Dr. Bob Boomer's 'better half'? What is the rest of my life for?"

Neither of the Boomers can really see themselves in a shuffleboard-and-golf style retirement, though Barb is tired to the point of exhaustion from the last two decades of trying to keep up with her adrenalin-addicted husband while also raising her three children, more or less single-handedly.

The Boomers are a fictional-real family, a composite of many different people I've worked with in the past, and their plight is typical of many people who have mistakenly identified their life purpose to only be about what they do to get by. We'll be following the Boomers as they travel along the Purposeful Path.

PREPARING
FOR THE JOURNEY

In preparing for this great journey along the Purposeful Path there are three major points to consider:

1. Where are you starting from?

2. What is your intended final destination?

3. What obstacles could prevent you from reaping the full benefit of your travels?

In question three, we're referring specifically to mental roadblocks that could come up before you even begin the adventure. So let's start by identifying three common obstacles, as well as a couple of ways to mentally prepare for the journey.

Having been a personal coach for over a decade and a half, I've come to realize that one of the ways I can add value to my clients' lives is by helping them to identify the blocks or obstacles that often prevent them from receiving the gift of wisdom that is constantly being offered to us. If you're reading this book, I am relating to you as one of my valued clients—and I invite you to relate to me as your coach, communicating to you through the pages of this book.

While it's true that tapping into our inner wisdom is a powerful means of bringing clarity to our lives, there's another resource many people fail to fully utilize. Oftentimes, we not only discount the wisdom coming from within, but we also construct mental roadblocks that prevent us from clearly hearing universal wisdom coming to us through other people. And though it may seem that these are two different problems, they are actually closely connected. When we remove the mental roadblocks, creating a clearer channel for receiving the contributions of others, we also begin to experience what resonates with our inner wisdom. How do we know what is resonating with our own truth? Keep what fits, and release the rest. But first we must eliminate the blocks that tend to prevent or distort the flow of wisdom.

God speaks to us in many ways, including through the voices of others—if only we will listen. Let's look at some of the mental blocks that may be preventing clear reception.

THE MAJOR OBSTACLES
ALONG THE PURPOSEFUL PATH

Monkey Mind

The mind creates 50,000 thoughts a day! The trick is not to become attached to any of them. These thoughts are simply the byproducts of the brain's metabolism, nothing to take too seriously.

The Buddhist term "monkey mind" is a poetic way of describing the mind's constant chatter. It refers to the little voice in your mind that comments on nearly everything you do or experience. It is that stream of consciousness that keeps flitting from one thing to another like a monkey jumping from branch to branch. Even when you are concentrating, your mind drifts off to fantasies about something you are going to do next weekend or an unresolved problem you must face tomorrow.

This chattering voice not only distracts you in most situations, but it also uses valuable brainpower. And if the ancient Buddhists had it bad, then monkey mind is an even bigger obstacle today with modern technology such as the television, radio, and the Internet reinforcing its constant chatter. We're constantly bombarded with input. And when we allow our actions to flow from the ramblings of the monkey mind, we become really blocked.

How many of us have been on a phone call when suddenly the monkey mind thinks, "I wonder what emails I've received?"

If we're not careful, before we know it, we're reading our email messages instead of listening to the person on the other end of the line. When our minds are chattering away it is nearly impossible to fully hear what another person is saying, and even harder to tune in to the subtle messages coming from God. How can we make sure these messages don't get lost in the noise? Well, for starters, just recognizing that we all have a monkey mind can help. By bringing it into our awareness, we can begin to tame the wild monkey. For instance, as soon as you notice you're listening to your monkey mind rather than the person you're talking with, you can stop and bring yourself back to the conversation. You may even want to ask the person to back up and repeat what they were saying before the monkey mind took over.

Taking time once or twice a day to quiet the mind can also prove very helpful in the long run. Meditation, reflection, or prayer can quiet the restless nature of your mind. If you find your mind chattering away at a time you can't slip away to meditate, take a moment to simply focus on your breathing. Eckhart Tolle, author of *The Power of Now*, observes that this simple process will help you return to your "inner body," quiet the mind, and bring yourself back to the present moment.

Another useful strategy is to periodically dump all the thoughts you've been trying to remember onto a sheet of paper. This can help free you from the monkey mind. As productivity guru David Allen points out in his book *Getting Things Done*, our ability to be productive, which includes hearing the voice of God coming from others, is directly proportional to our ability to relax. Only when our minds are clear and our thoughts are organized can we achieve a new level of stress-free productivity. Most of us try to hold way too much in our memories.

So, try dumping out all those thoughts onto a pad of paper. Write down all the appointments you've been trying to remember, the projects and next actions you need to take. Watch the monkey mind as it relaxes and becomes quiet. Then listen. There may be a message from God waiting for you.

The Full Cup Syndrome

Our second mental block is commonly called the full cup syndrome. It's best described by the following story from the Zen tradition:

> It appears a young seeker of wisdom traveled to the remote reaches of the world to learn enlightenment from the master. But before the master would even consider teaching him, he invited the young man to participate in the tea ceremony.
>
> So, they retired to the tea garden where the master began the much-venerated tea ceremony, preparing the water mindfully, adding the tea leaves just so. The master began pouring the tea into the young seeker's cup, talking politely as he did so. As the cup began to fill, the student-to-be grew nervous, yet the master continued to pour. The cup filled to the brim, and then the tea began to pour over.
>
> "Master, master," cried the young man, "you are overfilling my cup."
>
> Finally, with a smile, the master stopped pouring the tea. "Yes, and you are like the cup—so full of your own views and opinions there is no room for enlightenment."

Listening as though you already know everything that is being said is the listening of an already full cup, and it gets in the way receiving the contributions of others. This can also happen with material that you read, including this story about the seeker of wisdom and his Zen master. It's been around for quite a while. If you've heard it before, it would be easy to skip over the story this time and miss a deeper understanding of how it might apply to your life.

While it may sound amazing, I've found the full cup syndrome to be present even in coaching relationships. Imagine paying someone to coach you in your life, and then mentally coming to the coaching session so full that there's no room for any new insights. It happens. I may be particularly sensitive to this obstacle because it was one of the largest ones I've had to contend with in my own life. In fact, it continues to be so. I've crafted the Full Cup Syndrome into a work of art. If I'm not fully awake and aware, it's easy for me to enter into conversation thinking something like, "I not only know it all, but if you'll shut up for a moment, I'll tell you how it really is."

Whenever we come to a relationship as a full cup, there's very little opportunity for learning anything new or gaining insights that might make a difference. But interestingly enough, awareness goes a long way toward eliminating this mental roadblock. Once we notice that we're listening as though we already know everything, we can catch it and let it go. We can then begin to relate to the person who's trying to contribute in a different way. We'll explore some of these other ways later in this chapter.

Bias

Let's face it, we are all biased about something. We all have unexamined notions, assumptions, and beliefs, some of which often masquerade as truth. We bring these biases with us to any new relationship—often without even noticing we're doing it, because we do it so often that our bias is simply part of the background noise of our lives. And if we're not mindful, the unexamined notions, assumptions, and beliefs that make up our biases will effectively prevent us from evolving and growing from our interactions with others.

In other words, anything that doesn't fit in our normal paradigm or worldview will be discounted, ignored, glossed over, or rejected. An important part of coaching is revealing these previously unexamined notions, assumptions, and beliefs—particularly the ones that are viewed as simply "the way life is."

But how can we detect these biases when they stand in our way and threaten to prevent us from getting the most out of life? For starters, we can begin to notice our responses to other people. Often, when we hear a viewpoint or opinion that doesn't match our own, we react, sometimes quite strongly. When we're operating from our bias, we often listen to see if we agree or disagree with what the person is saying. And the more strongly we disagree, the more sacred the "truth" is that's being called into question.

Now, I'm not suggesting that you should simply accept everything anyone says as true. That would be erring at the other end of the spectrum. The starting point once again is awareness. Once again, begin by noticing your reactions. Do you tend to listen to see if you agree or disagree with what the other person is saying? If so, that's a good indication that a bias may be interfering with your ability to fully hear what's being said.

For example, clients often come to me convinced that "life is hard." For them it's not something they believe, it's a fact of life. It's often an ingrained family belief, passed on from one generation to another without anyone ever questioning it. Why should they? Look at all the evidence they have from decade after decade—life is hard!

It's important to realize that as human beings we have a tremendous power to co-create our reality with the divine source of it all. Unfortunately, we often abuse this creative ability by making ourselves right about our beliefs, including the beliefs that ultimately do not enhance our lives.

Bonus Coaching Assignment: Make a list of the "misbeliefs" that you hold as true and that do not enhance life. Begin to punch holes in the evidence you've accumulated to prove your misbelief.

The key to releasing each of these mental blocks—monkey mind, the full cup syndrome, and bias—is awareness. When we become aware that these mental blocks exist in all of us, we can then begin to be responsible for them. This makes it possible to set them aside and to design new ways of thinking that will enhance the value we can receive from others. What naturally begins to occur is a new opening for being fully present, aware, and available for contribution.

Beginner's Mind

Buddhists refer to this open-minded approach to life as "beginner's mind." Coming to a coaching relationship with a beginner's mind approach can make it possible for you to gain much more value from the coaching relationship. Of course, it's also important for the coach to come to the relationship in this open-minded fashion, ready to explore and examine with his or her client the various aspects and dimensions of life.

With a beginner's mind, you're not discounting or ignoring the work you've already done in life or the wisdom you've gleaned up to this point. You're simply willing to build upon this foundation, to take it into account, and yet not be limited by it.

Turning On Your Radar for Insights

When you come to a conversation with a beginner's mind you are open and receptive to insight. Your mind becomes a radar. Its job is to pick up useful and valuable insights that will contribute to your life. One definition of insight is, "the act or result of apprehending the inner nature of things or of seeing intuitively." But detecting insights is just the first step.

Look at the following formula, which my first coach, Judy Billman, shared with me. See if you can fill in the missing part of the equation:

Insight + _____ = True Growth and Development

Judy pointed out to me that it's easy to become overly enamored with insights. While, as the formula suggests, insights are an important part of our growing and developing as human beings, they aren't all that powerful by themselves. Or, as Judy used to say, "Insights by themselves are a bit like a pinch in the buttocks. They may be momentarily interesting, but hardly life transforming." So what's the missing part of the equation? What is necessary in order for our insights to contribute to our lives?

The answer is action. In other words, we need to integrate the insights we glean from coaching conversations into our lives through action. By the way, virtually any conversation can be viewed as a coaching conversation when you keep the monkey mind, full cup syndrome, and bias out of the way. One simple way to do this is to write your insights down on the Insight Pages you will find at the end of the book. Then, periodically, take an insight that resonates with where you are and determine what action or actions you will take to begin to integrate it into your life.

A Word about Call to Action Assignments

One of the easiest ways to sabotage your travels along the Purposeful Path—and greatly reduce the value you receive from your journey—is not completing the assignments that are posted along the way. It is by fully committing the Call to Action Assignments that you will integrate your insights into your everyday life. So take the time to complete the assignments, especially the ones that you're inclined to "come back to later."

DETERMINING YOUR STARTING POINT

Let's imagine for the moment that we want to travel across the United States to San Francisco. What route would you likely take? Before you can really answer that question, you need to know the answer to another question: Where are you starting from?

In other words, it is important to determine where you presently are in your life so you'll have a clearer sense of where the Purposeful Path may lead. You'll do this using three purpose tools—the Life on Purpose Scale, the Living on Purpose Self-Test, and the Wheel of Life. With the Life on Purpose Scale you'll be able to gauge how clear or unclear you are about your life purpose. The Living on Purpose Self-Test will help you determine how on or off-purpose your life is presently, while the Wheel of Life will give you a good overview and visual of your present life. From these exercises, you'll have a clear picture of your current reality.

Awareness Alert! There may be a tendency to pass judgment on yourself as you evaluate where you presently are in your life. Remember, there's no right or wrong place to be. You simply are where you are. So, as you use these purpose tools, just be honest and authentic with yourself without being overly critical.

The Life on Purpose Scale

Let's start the process of getting a clear picture of your current reality using the Life on Purpose Scale, which will give you an initial benchmark of how clear you are about your life purpose. Avoid the temptation to criticize or judge yourself. Be honest as well as gentle as you assess yourself.

In regards to your life purpose, circle the one statement that best describes where you are in understanding and living true to your life purpose:

A. I have no idea what my purpose in life is, not a clue.

B. I have a vague idea of what my life purpose is, but I need to be much clearer.

C. I have a fairly good idea what my life purpose is.

D. I am clear what my life purpose is, but I am not living consistent with it.

E. I am certain of my life purpose and live consistent with it about 25% of the time.

F. I am certain of my life purpose and live consistent with it about 50% of the time.

G. I am certain of my life purpose and live consistent with it about 75% of the time.

H. I am certain of my life purpose and I live consistent with it 100% of the time.

Now, let's get specific about your life purpose. Give your most authentic description of what you consider your life purpose to be. And don't worry, it's impossible to get it wrong. We'll revisit your response later, after we've traveled further down the Purposeful Path.

My life purpose is:

_____

_____

_____

EXERCISE: LIVING ON PURPOSE SELF-TEST

The following exercise, known as the Life on Purpose Self-Test, will help you determine where you are today so you'll know your starting point along the Purposeful Path.

Why is this important? Think of it this way. Have you ever gone into a large shopping mall and needed to find a new store, but you didn't know where in the mall it was located? What did you do? Perhaps you wandered around for quite some time trying to find the shop. Or maybe you asked someone else in the mall. Or perhaps you went to one of the directories usually located at each entrance.

If you chose this last option, you probably found an X on that map, with a note saying "You are Here," or something to that effect. Map designers know that it's easier to find where you want to go if you start by knowing where you are. And that's what you'll be doing with this fun and engaging self-test.

Note: If you prefer, you may also take the self-test online at www. lifeonpurpose.com/selftest. The online version will automatically score your results.

Step One

Circle the number that represents how strongly you resonate with each of the following statements. Use five as neutral. Anything below five isn't working or lacks clarity; above five is working above average or is clear.

1. I am crystal clear about what my life purpose is.

    Disagree   1   2   3   4   5   6   7   8   9   10   Agree

2. The life I lead is a full expression of my life purpose. (Of course, you need to know your purpose for your life to be an expression of it.)

    Disagree   1   2   3   4   5   6   7   8   9   10   Agree

3. My life purpose is designed to nurture me and those around me.

   Disagree 1 2 3 4 5 6 7 8 9 10 Agree

4. My life purpose gives me plenty of room to fully express myself.

   Disagree 1 2 3 4 5 6 7 8 9 10 Agree

5. Those around me fully know and relate to me in accordance with my life purpose.

   Disagree 1 2 3 4 5 6 7 8 9 10 Agree

6. I recognize the contribution I make to others by expressing my life purpose.

   Disagree 1 2 3 4 5 6 7 8 9 10 Agree

7. I live a values-based life rather than a materialistic life.

   Disagree 1 2 3 4 5 6 7 8 9 10 Agree

8. My life is shaped by my life purpose rather than by what others expect of me or think I should be.

   Disagree 1 2 3 4 5 6 7 8 9 10 Agree

9. I fully experience and am grateful for the simple abundance all around me.

   Disagree 1 2 3 4 5 6 7 8 9 10 Agree

10. My life is free of unnecessary clutter and complexities and I seldom feel overwhelmed, rushed, or cluttered.

    Disagree 1 2 3 4 5 6 7 8 9 10 Agree

11. I regularly acknowledge the gracious bounty of my life.

    Disagree   1   2   3   4   5   6   7   8   9   10   Agree

12. I fully realize that many of the best things in life are free, and my life reflects this.

    Disagree   1   2   3   4   5   6   7   8   9   10   Agree

13. I trust that as I live true to my purpose the Universe will provide everything I need for the expression of that purpose.

    Disagree   1   2   3   4   5   6   7   8   9   10   Agree

14. I regularly take time to nurture myself in ways that feed my soul.

    Disagree   1   2   3   4   5   6   7   8   9   10   Agree

15. I have plenty of time to devote to my family, friends, and community.

    Disagree   1   2   3   4   5   6   7   8   9   10   Agree

16. I have a rich and satisfying spiritual life.

    Disagree   1   2   3   4   5   6   7   8   9   10   Agree

17. I have taken time to explore my beliefs to be certain they are of my own choice, rather than what others think I should believe.

    Disagree   1   2   3   4   5   6   7   8   9   10   Agree

18. I've established my home as a sanctuary for the soul.

    Disagree   1   2   3   4   5   6   7   8   9   10   Agree

19. I feel a deep sense of security and I'm seldom fearful of not having "enough" of anything.

    Disagree   1   2   3   4   5   6   7   8   9   10   Agree

20. I regularly reach out to assist others on their paths to living on purpose.

    Disagree   1   2   3   4   5   6   7   8   9   10   Agree

Step Two

Now add up your total score and write it down here: _____
Your answer should be somewhere between 20 and 200.

Step Three

The last step is to determine which of the following categories describes where you are right now. Pick the range your score falls into. Before doing so, remember that the point of the exercise is simply to get an idea of where you're starting. There is no right or wrong place to be any more than there's a right or wrong entrance to the mall. Be careful not to disempower yourself with unnecessary judgments.

20–50: Adrift

Your life is like a rudderless boat cast adrift at sea, tossed about by the turbulent currents of circumstance. You might view this self-test as a wake up call. Life has so much more to offer than you are currently experiencing. Sure, it might feel at this point that you have to pull yourself up by your own bootstraps, but this isn't necessarily the case. Look around. The Universe is waiting to provide you with whatever you need. The trick is to start today—right now in the moment. What one action could you take to live more fully on purpose? Who could you call upon for help and support? What requests could you make that would begin the process of healing and nurturing your soul?

51–80: Surviving

At this level you're getting by in your life, although many times it may feel like something is missing. Those feelings could be your soul beginning to awaken to the rich possibilities that lie ahead. Trust those feelings and begin to ask your inner guidance system for what's needed to begin fulfilling your life. To do this, you'll need time for quiet reflection. Carving out this time in your life will be richly rewarding, especially if you then follow the suggestions that arise from these moments.

81–110: Striving

Your life is moving forward well at this level and you have much to be thankful for, although you may not be fully aware of these blessings. So, a little gratitude work can go a long way in moving you to the next level. Two ideal times to consciously practice gratitude are in the morning, as you first awaken, and at night, as you prepare for sleep. If you haven't already done so, consider starting a gratitude journal, or simply devote five to ten minutes in the morning and evening to counting your blessings. It'll be time well spent.

111–140: Competency

Congratulations! You've been doing good work in your life and it shows. You're living a life that works and that has integrity, and you're reaping the bounty of such a life. People and opportunities are beginning to be naturally attracted to you. It's now time to take on a renewed sense of responsibility in your life. You are a light, a beacon for what's possible. In owning this, you move forward in your life as well as becoming an inspiration for others. To go to the next level, let your light shine. Share your gifts, your blessings, and your truest nature with others—not boastfully, but authentically.

141–170: Flourishing

Cherish your life. You have created it as a sanctuary for your soul as well as for those around you. Your life is like a tranquil harbor where others can come to rest and receive support. At the same time, you know your true self well enough to speak the truth in a way that contributes to others. Going to the next level involves trusting yourself, your inner guidance, and the Universe.

171–200: Mastery

One of the signs of being a master is knowing that one is never fully a master of anything. However, at this level you are comfortable with such a paradox. Now it is time to give away all that you have learned, knowing that you can never out-give the Universe — for the more you give, the more the Universe provides.

Step Four

As you continue to travel along the Purposeful Path, monitor your progress by repeating the self-test about every three months. This will give you the opportunity to notice the progress you're making as well as to distinguish areas in which to focus more attention.

Taking a Closer Look at the Self-Test

Let's spend a few minutes taking a closer look at the self-test statements so you can begin to see how each of them fits into a Life on Purpose.

1. I am crystal clear about what my life purpose is.

The truth is, most people aren't clear what their life purpose is, even though they think they are. In fact, according to the popular book *Cool Careers for Dummies*, 46% of men and 40% of women say that they are still trying to figure out the meaning and purpose of their lives.

When William Marsten, a prominent psychologist, asked 3,000 people what they had to live for, 94% responded by saying they had no definite purpose for their lives—94%!

So why is it so important to be clear about your purpose? Think of your life purpose like a source of light. If you are clueless about your life purpose, the light is off and pretty much all you see is darkness. If you have a vague idea of what your life purpose is, then the light is like a tabletop lamp. It may be warm and comforting, but it still lacks power. But a crystal clear and focused life purpose is like the light of a laser beam, able to cut through the circumstances that often stop other people from living a satisfying and fulfilling life.

One of the first steps to becoming crystal clear about your life purpose is to determine how clear or unclear you are.

2. The life I lead is a full expression of my life purpose.

If you aren't clear about your life purpose, then, of course, you scored low on this statement. But being clear about your life purpose is really just the first leg along the Purposeful Path. The real journey begins when you begin to live and express your life purpose. That's why I consider the second stage of the Life on Purpose Process to be where the rubber meets the road. Otherwise the statement of your life purpose devolves into a "purpose platitude" with little if any influence on your day-to-day life.

Interestingly enough, you can begin today to start living true to your life purpose, even as you also continue to clarify what it is. We'll begin this process in the Creating the Gap exercise.

3. My life purpose is designed to nurture me and those around me.

I know this may sound strange, but some of the Life Purpose Statements people create are steeped in guilt, a sense of obligation, or even fear. They may feel that they were sent here to do something that only they can do, and so, if they're not doing it or being successful at it, then they feel guilty. This combo of obligation and guilt can be a real downer.

A few years ago I worked with a client—I'll call him Ed. When I asked him what his view of a life purpose was and what he felt his own life purpose was, he replied, "I think a life purpose is something that you were put on earth to do that only you can accomplish."

Ed went on to explain that several years before he had met a woman who he felt had some extraordinary insights into the spiritual realm. He and his wife had continued to meet in a group of others to listen to and discourse with this spiritual sage. Ed had received permission to record many of these meetings, with the intention of one day making the contents of those tapes available to the world.

He was the only person with this material at this point, he said, and he felt spreading the spiritual message of this sage was his life purpose. Unfortunately, he'd yet to do anything with the tapes, and so felt an incredible amount of guilt and remorse about not fulfilling his life purpose.

But I don't believe that a life of guilt and remorse is what God has intended for any of us. If the thought of your life purpose leaves you with these kinds of feelings, there are at least two different possible causes.

First, you may have misidentified your life purpose as something you should be doing, rather than something you're inspired to do. As you will discover in the Life on Purpose Process, your life purpose isn't ever about what you do, but is instead more about who you are. Your life purpose is never based in "shoulds." Shoulds come from conditioning; they are not the source of your true life purpose.

The other possible cause for feelings of guilt or remorse is if you have identified some aspect of your life purpose or some action that is an expression of your life purpose, but then fail to move forward. The only thing worse than never waking up to your life purpose is waking up to it and then not taking action to live true to it.

So, check in to see if you're experiencing any guilt or remorse about your life purpose. If so, ask yourself what these emotions trying to tell you about your life. Take some time to check in with your inner spirit to see what it has to say…then, follow its guidance.

Remember, your life purpose is meant to nourish and nurture you and others. If what you have identified as a life purpose isn't nourishing you at this point, be suspicious. It is either no longer your purpose in life, if it ever was, or it is a part of your life purpose that you've not been willing to act upon.

4. My life purpose gives me plenty of room to fully express myself.

While this may at first sound like a repeat of statement number two, there's a subtle yet important difference. Statement number two is about whether or not you're living your life purpose. Statement number four points to another quality of a life purpose.

A life purpose is focused and clear, yet at the same time it isn't constraining or limiting to the self or the soul. We'll talk more about the qualities to expect in a true life purpose in a later chapter.

5. Those around me fully know and relate to me in accordance with my life purpose.

This statement points to the relational aspect of being human. The more people know you and relate to you in accordance with your life purpose, the more freely you can express it in the world. Thus, the longer you live true to your life purpose, the easier it gets, especially if you're sharing who you are with the people in your life.

Said another way, your life purpose doesn't just live inside you. If it does, it has a very real chance of being stifled out of existence. For your life purpose to flourish it needs room to breathe in the consciousness of other people. The more people who know what your life purpose is and who relate to you, at least in part, as that life purpose, the more room you have to play and express yourself consistently with your life purpose.

So, as you journey along the Purposeful Path, be sure you're sharing yourself with others. Besides, it's always fun to have other people along for the ride.

6. I recognize the contribution I make to others by expressing my life purpose.

Your life purpose in action is a contribution. Inherent in being human is a deep-seated desire to make a difference with other human beings. We long to contribute, to be of service, and when we're living true to our life purpose, being of service is a natural byproduct. Another way to say this is that your life purpose isn't just about you—it includes you and others as well.

As you become clear about what your purpose in life is, you will discover new and inventive ways to express that purpose in all areas of your life. You no longer have to think about your life purpose only in terms of your job, career, or profession. Nor do you need to limit it to the roles you play in life, such as being the best parent you can be, a loving sibling, or good employee.

It really is possible to be your life purpose in all areas of your life, to literally live true to your life purpose 100% of the time. Now, for many people, that may seem to be a distant goal, far down the Purposeful Path; but that's okay, because the journey to that destination is fun and exciting.

As you travel along the Purposeful Path and become clearer about your life purpose, stop from time to time to ponder how, where, and with whom you would enjoy contributing to others. Often this step will help lead you to clarifying your life purpose. Why? Because the contributions we make are like breadcrumbs of passion, bits of information and feelings that lead us to our true purpose and calling.

7. I live a values-based life rather than a materialistic life.

In today's times, this can be a difficult statement to live up to. Our Western culture is so heavily steeped in materialism that it's difficult to not get caught up in it. We're assaulted every day with hundreds if not thousands of invitations to buy more, more, more. It's easy to get confused and think that our life purpose is about having more rather than about being.

I'm not saying there's anything wrong with "stuff," or the desire to have material possessions. Part of my own life purpose is living a life of "mindful abundance and simplicity." I stand for and believe that we all live in a bountiful and abundant universe, and that God provides us with all the resources we need to live and express our true purpose. But we run into a problem and risk getting bumped off the Purposeful Path when we base our lives on our desire for stuff rather than on our true values—those intangibles that motivate us to serve and live true to our purpose.

Begin this week to get in touch with your true, core values. What really does matter most to you in life? What would you really desire to have more of in your life? What could there be more of to make the world a better place in which to live?

Then ask yourself, "Where is my life being shaped by my values, and where is it being shaped by my need for more stuff?" How might your life change if you used your values as the truing mechanism to keep you on track? What actions could you take this week to start aligning your life to your values?

8. My life is shaped by my life purpose rather than by what others expect of me or think I should be.

We'll learn as we travel further along the Purposeful Path that obligations and the expectations of others are two powerful influences that can keep us stuck in the rut of living a life off purpose.

This is particularly true when we aren't clear about who we are and why we're here, when we don't know what we stand for in life. As the old saying goes, "If you don't know what you stand for, you'll fall for anything." When we begin to examine our life more closely, we'll likely find places where it is being shaped by the expectations of people who aren't even a part of our life anymore. This may include deceased parents, divorced spouses, former employers, and long lost friends.

I've been an orphan for a number of years now. My dad died when I was six, and my mother passed on over five years ago. While I love them both, I realize that I'm unwilling to have their expectations of me continue to shape my life. And the truth is, I don't think they really expect anything of me at this point!

Once we recognize that we've been giving our power to other people, we can begin to reassess the situation. Perhaps it's time to take some if not all of that power back.

Where have you given away your power and the choices to design your own life to the expectations of others, living or dead? What action could you take this week to reclaim some of that lost power?

9. I fully experience and am grateful for the simple abundance all around me.

It's such a powerful phrase—"simple abundance." Can we ever fully experience the joy that can be found in such abundance all around us? I think not. I don't believe there's any ceiling on experiencing this joy, especially since many of us experience so little of what's actually possible. Because it's so easy to get caught up in our cultural obsessions of doing and having, we often miss the joy of just being—being in nature, being with ourselves, being with our loved ones.

When did you last take the time to just listen to the birds in the early morning hours as the sun began to rise? Or to study the fresh green leaves as they first started to emerge in the spring? Or, took the time to tiptoe into your children's bedroom at night and watch them sleep?

As I was writing this, I looked up for a moment from my work. Outside, in the trees near my bird feeder, I saw a pair of Cardinals and a redheaded woodpecker flitting from branch to branch. A chickadee joined them. In your life, do you take the time to experience such simple abundance throughout your day? Where could you take the time—even ten to fifteen minutes, two or three times during your day—to appreciate the simple abundance all around you?

10. My life is free of unnecessary clutter and complexities, and I seldom feel overwhelmed, rushed, or cluttered.

If you rated yourself low on this one, you're far from alone. Thousands of people have completed the Life on Purpose Self-Test via our web site, and this statement has consistently been the one on which people score lowest.

It's not really surprising when you think of our cultural obsession with frenetic doingness. Overwhelmed, rushed, and cluttered is the norm. In fact, we often wear these vestiges of busyness like a badge of courage. We say, "Oh, I'm sorry, my calendar is filled up for the next three weeks," when we're really not sorry. We're proud. We're up to something big. But is it, really? Maybe yes, maybe no.

Is it possible to live on purpose and not have to be so busy that we don't even have time to clean up our clutter, to simplify our lives both in the realms of doing and having? I suggest that it is possible. Keeping our lives simple may not always be easy, but it's worth the extra effort.

I encourage you to take a few minutes today to explore your life. How cluttered or uncluttered is it? Where could you simplify your life, and in so doing, create more space to be? Don't look just in the physical realm of stuff. Look also in your thoughts. Is your mind overly cluttered with upsets, resentments, and guilt from the past? How much room in your mental attic are these unproductive thoughts taking up? And how about your daily activity? Do you schedule time for yourself, to give nourishment to your soul as well as your body and ego?

What one action could you take this week to free yourself from these various forms of clutter? What are you doing that doesn't support who you are? Could you eliminate it now? Eliminating the clutter and complexities will open up more room to discover who you really are.

11. I regularly acknowledge the gracious bounty of my life.

Gratitude—so simple and powerful, yet so often under utilized. How many of us shrug off the old adage to "count your blessings" as old-fashioned?

If you don't regularly acknowledge the bounty of your life, you're simply missing a great opportunity to gently and graciously add immense value to the quality of living. If you don't believe me, try this simple experiment. For the next thirty days, finish off each day with gratitude. You can either write down the ten things that you're most grateful for from the day, or even simpler, just count your blessings as you fall asleep. If you catch yourself having other thoughts, especially thoughts about what went wrong during the day or worries about the following day, stop, breathe, and go back to counting your blessings.

12. I fully realize that many of the best things in life are free, and my life reflects this.

This realization is a great compliment to the gratitude exercises I suggested. In our materialistic culture, it's easy to forget that some of the best things in life don't cost a dime. How much are a sincere hug and kiss from a child worth? They're priceless—and free for the asking. Do you own a pet? When was the last time you spent an evening with the television off, brushing and massaging your dog or cat, or romping around the house with him?

Of course, I could go on and on, pointing out the endless number of free gifts we're presented with each day. See if you can make your own list. Spend the next few days finding or creating as many wonderful free gifts as you can. And if you want to play the bonus round, introduce those around you to this game, particularly anyone who seems to be caught up in a mindset of lack or scarcity.

13. I trust that, as I live true to my purpose, the Universe will provide everything I need for the expression of that purpose.

Now we're getting into the meat of living on purpose: trust! Trusting ourselves, trusting others, and most of all, trusting God. Trust can be a big issue for many of us. And, as this statement suggests, a deep and abiding trust is paramount to our experiencing heaven on earth. When we trust, we attract all the resources necessary to live and express our true purpose for being here. Have you ever wondered why we sometimes receive missions or callings that seem to our small minds to be utterly impossible to accomplish? What if it's because God wants to be involved in our lives by assisting us in fulfilling these "impossible" missions?

Where have you blocked the bountiful resources of God's universe with boulders of distrust? What could life be like if you did truly believe and trust unequivocally that God is prepared to completely support you in living your true purpose in life? What small steps could you take this week toward developing more trust and faith? Remember what the Bible says about the power of a mustard seed's worth of faith: "And Jesus said unto them, Because of your unbelief: for verily I say unto you, If ye have faith as a grain of *mustard seed*, ye shall say unto this mountain, Remove hence to yonder place; and it shall remove; and nothing shall be impossible unto you." *(Mt 17:20)*

14. I regularly take time to nurture myself in ways that feed my soul.

Are you feeding your soul a balanced diet, or are you trying to nurture it with junk food? Junk food is so bad for our bodies because it is not nutritionally balanced. Most of it has too much sugar and other starches, and not enough protein, vitamins, or minerals.

Many people feed their souls junk food by living lives that are out of balance. They strive to achieve status and accumulate things, and overlook the essential ingredients of being and experiencing life fully. When we feed our bodies nothing but junk food, it doesn't matter how much of it we eat; our bodies will never be fully nourished and satisfied because some key ingredients are missing. Likewise, no matter how much more you do or strive to have, your soul will never be truly nourished.

The good news is that, just like our bodies really know what they need to stay healthy, so do our souls—if we'll take the time to listen. For the next few days, why not try this out and see what you discover. Schedule a few minutes each morning to get in touch with your soul and ask it what it needs to feel nurtured and cared for. Then supply what it needs. Who knows, you may become addicted to feeding your soul a healthy, nutritious life.

15. I have plenty of time to devote to my family, friends, and community.

When people are interviewed at the end of their life and asked what they wished they'd had more time for, no one says they wish they'd spent more time at work. Instead, people say they wish they'd devoted more time with their family, friends, and loved ones.

What does that tell those of us who still have time left here on Earth? This is a tough one for me because I love my work. I love being a Life Purpose Coach and running Life on Purpose Institute. It's easy to let it consume my life, but if I do then what do I miss out on? I'm lucky in one sense because my wife, Ann, works closely with me at Life on Purpose Institute, so we get to spend more time together than if she wasn't involved. Still, there's life outside of even the most meaningful work.

When my daughter, Amber, turned thirteen, Ann and I began to worry that she would be grown up before we knew it. I see my daughter a lot more than some parents, because I work from my home. But I can still miss out on really being with her unless I consciously create opportunities.

Ann and I homeschool Amber. She loves being at home and tends to learn better in this more casual setting. On the one hand, I wonder how I'm going to maintain my coaching practice and Life on Purpose Institute while being an active part of Amber's schooling. But deep down inside I know it's right for both of us. I know that it will be good for me as a coach and as the director of the Life on Purpose Institute, because being one of her teachers has integrity for me. I think it will actually allow me to be more effective and efficient at work. It will motivate me to delegate and empower people around me to do some of the work that I was previously afraid to give away.

You see, I don't want get to the end of my life and regret that I didn't spend more time with my loved ones. I'm out to live a life with no regrets. I don't quite know how I'm going to pull it off, but I know that trust is key. I know I can trust God to show me how to be an effective coach, a powerful director of Life on Purpose Institute, and a proactive and involved husband, parent, and teacher.

How about you? What would a life with no regrets look and feel like for you?

16. I have a rich and satisfying spiritual life.

Many of us grew up in the American culture that told us that a "rich spiritual life" meant attending church services every Sunday, whether or not it fed our spirit. Of course that gave us a reprieve from thinking about God or spirit for the rest of the week.

I feel that, in many ways, the United States and much of the rest of the world is in the midst of a spiritual awakening. Many of us former closet-spiritual types are coming out and being much more public about our strong beliefs in a higher power. And there is a rich tapestry of different ways to express our spiritual nature.

Since the idea of living on purpose means to experience a rewarding and satisfying life, it's only natural to include our spiritual nature in the mix. How one does this is really up to each individual, as long as it doesn't infringe on the spiritual freedom of another. If you found as you went through the self-test that your spiritual nature is starving for some loving attention, then please pay attention to this wake-up call.

You may want to start by returning to whatever religious or spiritual roots you had growing up. You may want to start fresh and explore several paths until you find the one that resonates most strongly with your soul. The important thing is to watch for the signs of a spirit longing to be awakened.

17. I have taken time to explore my beliefs to be certain they are of my own choice, rather than what others think I should believe.

Here is why choosing our beliefs is so important. What we believe is what shapes our experience of reality. If you believe in scarcity and lack, you will experience a world in which there is never enough money, time, or good relationship to go around. Nothing, including you, will ever be good enough.

Many people haven't taken the time and done the inner work to identify what they truly believe. Without this work, you are a product of the beliefs that were instilled in you long ago. Even when you consciously select your beliefs, some maintenance work is required to ensure that those beliefs continue to serve you. Otherwise, before you know it, some out-dated belief will seep into your subconscious and begin to create an experience of reality that simply doesn't enhance your life.

I suggest making it a common practice to identify at least one belief each week that doesn't serve you in living a Life on Purpose. Then, go to work to weed it out from your consciousness and choose a new belief to take its place. In one sense, much of the Life on Purpose Process operates at this level, assisting you to identify old, life draining, fear-based beliefs and then allowing you to choose new, life-enhancing, love-based beliefs. As you do this, you transform your life into a Life on Purpose.

18. I've established my home as a sanctuary for the soul.

Our outer environment often reflects our inner environment and vice versa. So, if you want your outer environment to support your commitment to living a Life on Purpose, do the work to have it reflect your life purpose. If you accept that your life purpose is your spirit's reason for being on earth, then you will want your home and surroundings to be a sanctuary for the soul.

Of course, this will look different for different people. For example, it's not by accident that I live in the Blue Ridge Mountains of North Carolina. Where I live is by design, because it supports me in living a life of service, simplicity, and spiritual serenity. My wife and I took a year and a half asking ourselves the question, "If we could live anywhere we wanted to, where would we choose to live?" It was a fun time as we explored many different locations, but we kept returning to this area. I had always been drawn to the mountains, as had my wife. We wanted to live close to where her family lives so that our daughter would have the experience of growing up knowing her grandmother and great-grandmother. The location we picked is in the heart of the mountains and only forty minutes from Ann's family.

Once you have chosen a place to live, make sure your immediate surroundings nurture your spirit. A couple of years ago, I spent a good part of my summer building a meditation pond in our back yard. Not only was the project a lot of fun, but we now have a very quiet, spiritual place to rest and meditate. In fact, much of this book was written while I sat around the pond, listening to the water flow over the rocks of the waterfall.

What steps could you take this week to create your surroundings as a sanctuary for the soul? Eliminating clutter or unnecessary stuff that will free up space is a good place to start.

19. I feel a deep sense of security and I'm seldom fearful of not having "enough" of anything.

This can be a tough one for many people. One of the side effects of living in such a materialistic society is that many of us often feel deprived if we don't have all the things that the advertisers spend billions of dollars trying to convince us we can't live without. This can spawn a sense of lack or scarcity based in fear.

When you live true to your purpose, you begin to experience a dramatic shift in your experience of life. It's not that you don't continue to have desires. You will. However, you are better able to separate your true desires from what others think you should want or shouldn't live without. It is important to understand the distinctions between the two. The word "desire" comes from the Latin *desidarare*, "from the father" or "from the heavens"—so true desires are gifts from God that are consistent with living on purpose. It is possible to desire something while at the same time being free and unattached from "needing" it. Whereas your wants can often bump you off the Purposeful Path, your desires can help to guide you along.

20. I regularly reach out to assist others on their paths to living on purpose.

In one sense, we're all on a Purposeful Path. Some are sleep walking along, while others are in the process of awakening to what's possible. Others may be quite a way down the path. Wherever you are in your journey, you can reach out and assist others. Stopping to help someone else doesn't slow you down. Just the opposite. It's one of the many Purposeful Paradoxes you will find along the Purposeful Path.

Who could you assist along the way this week? Reach out a helping hand and see what happens.

EXERCISE: WHEEL OF LIFE

This is a fun, engaging, and revealing exercise, so take your time doing it. As you continue to explore what shapes your life, this exercise will help to give you a visual representation of how it looks in the present.

Step One

Make a list of the primary areas of your life. Include all the areas of importance so that your whole life is represented. There will probably be from five to ten different areas. For example, your list may include work, family, recreation, spirituality, community, and so on. Pick the areas and the terms that work best for you.

Area of Life	Working	Satisfied	Average

Step Two

On a scale of one to ten (1 = unsatisfactory and 10 = great), evaluate where you presently are in each area of your life. Consider each from the following two perspectives, then take the average of both:

- The degree to which life is working in that area
- The degree to which you are satisfied and fulfilled in that area

For example, your career might be working just fine. You're getting your job done, your employer is pleased...and yet you're not satisfied or fulfilled. So, it might be working at the level of an eight, but the degree of satisfaction is at a four. Your final evaluation for that area would be around a six (8+4=12÷2=6).

Step Three

Once you have your list, use the wheel below to create a visual representation of your life. For each area of life, draw a line from the hub of the wheel to the outer rim for each area on your list. At the outer rim where the line connects, write the word or phrase that that line represents.

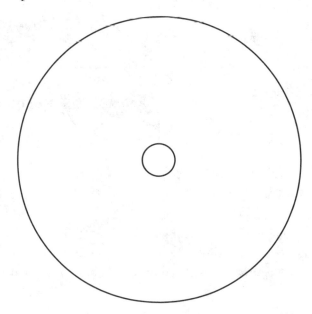

Step Four

Write each of the numbers from the average column of your table on the lines or spokes that represents their specific area, with the hub representing a zero, five in the middle of the spoke, and ten at the rim.

Step Five

Once you've completed the evaluation for all the areas, play "connect the numbers." Draw a line from one number to the next until you have all the numbers connected, which will give you an inner circle or wheel.

Take a look at your wheel. Is it balanced? Would your ride be bumpy or smooth if this wheel were on your car? What does this inner circle reveal about your life?

Wheel of Life Example

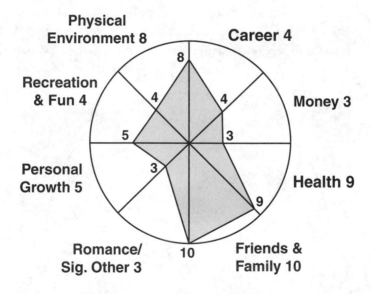

Does your wheel of life look like one of the spare tires that many cars come with these days—the ones that are considerably smaller than the other tires on your car? While these smaller spares will get you to a service station, you wouldn't want to travel very far with one of them on your car.

It's not unusual for people to find that their wheel of life is much the same. It's not that their life is really out of balance, but it's much smaller than it should or *could* be. One of my clients reported that her wheel was in good balance, but that she scored most of her areas in the four-to-five category. While this insight was a bit uncomfortable for her at first, she used it to her advantage and committed to "pump some life" into her life.

Remember, your life is not a dress rehearsal, nor is it meant to be the size of a spare tire. It can be as full and as fulfilling as you're willing to make it. The interesting thing about this, as we'll continue to learn, is that pumping up your life doesn't necessary mean you need to add more to do to it. In many cases, just the opposite may be true.

Most people fail to realize that their feelings toward others are determined by their feelings towards themselves.

—Sydney J. Harris

DETERMINING YOUR DESTINATION

The next important part of preparing for a journey is determining your destination—which, in the case of this journey along the Purposeful Path, means getting a clear sense of what your Life on Purpose will be like. We'll look at the top ten benefits that others who have traveled along the Purposeful Path ahead of you have reported receiving. Using this information, you'll begin to create a "visionary reality" of what your Life on Purpose will be like.

The Top Ten Benefits to Knowing and Living Your Purpose

As you read over these top ten benefits, pick three or four that feel most important to include in your Life on Purpose. At the end of this list, there will be an important assignment to complete.

Benefit #1—Focus

When you clearly know your life purpose, it becomes a truing mechanism that allows you to focus more clearly on what matters most to you. Many people report that this has been one of the most valuable benefits of going through the Purpose Process, because once they found their focus, they could begin to use their life purpose to make their decisions about where and how to invest their time, energy, money, and talents.

Oftentimes, a life that is unfocused and scattered is a life off purpose, much like a boat without a rudder. When you don't know your true purpose in life, you tend to be thrown all over the place by the currents of circumstances.

Benefit #2—Passion

For many people, clarifying their life purpose becomes the key to unlocking their passion for life. Their passion then becomes the fuel that propels them forward. They act in extraordinary ways, surpassing anything they would have even imagined without the spark of their purpose. For inspiring stories straight out of the files of Project Purpose, go to the Life on Purpose Institute web site at: www.lifeonpurpose.com/projectpurpose.

A life off purpose is often devoid of any real passion. The experience can be a little bit like the movie Pleasantville. At the start of the movie, everyone in *Pleasantville* is living a dull, black and white life; but over time they begin to tap into their passion and learn that life can be a beautiful, multi-colored experience filled with passionate moments.

Benefit #3 — Becoming Unstoppable

The longer people live true to their purpose and the more they allow their purpose to shape their lives, the more unstoppable they become. Yet, at the same time, purposeful people aren't attached to their position. They have learned that it's not necessary to go through life like a bull, ramming through anything that tries to get in their way. They've found that a little patience, persistence, and surrender to the timeline of a higher power can go a long way.

People without clarity of purpose often find themselves stopped or stuck in life. Because they haven't tapped into their passion, they're like high-powered automobiles without any fuel in their tanks.

Benefit #4 — Fulfillment

Living a life in which you are regularly expressing your life purpose and allowing it to shape your decisions, thoughts, feelings, and actions is simply a whole lot more fulfilling. A Life on Purpose is filled with meaning, and people on purpose realize that they are making a difference simply by being in the world. Whatever they choose to do to express their life purpose is like icing on the cake.

People living off purpose often have a life filled with meaning as well. Unfortunately, the meaning that they choose to see stems from fear and preoccupies them with the need to struggle and suffer. It helps to remember that although pain may be inevitable, suffering is optional. Knowing your purpose is the key to making this important shift.

Benefit #5 — Value-based Living

You will learn as you delve deeper into the Purpose Process that one integral component of a person's life purpose is their core values — those intangibles of life that mean the most to them. Our core values are at the heart of all the values we've been taught we "should" value.

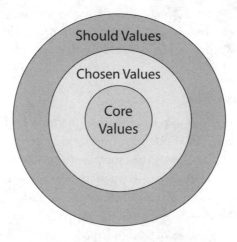

Think of it like three concentric circles: The largest circle is composed of our "should" values; the next circle inside that one is our "chosen" values—the should values that we actually choose to hold onto and live from; and the last circle is our "core" values—those chosen values that truly matter most to us. Since these core values are an integral part of a life purpose, when you live a Life on Purpose, you are living a value-based life, rather than one that is lifestyle-based.

People living off purpose are often focused on living more from the outer circle of their "should" values, what often is described as "keeping up with the Joneses." In a lifestyle-based life, the focus is on life looking a certain way—the way we were taught our life was supposed to look. The focus is often more on stuff and on doing what's expected of us, not on what gives us the most joy.

Benefit #6—Fun

Let's face it, living on purpose is simply a lot more fun than living a life based in fear and obligations. People who know and are living true to their life purpose have a renewed zest for life. They can bring purposeful play to almost any situation and find or create ways for each day to be a reflection of their true joy and purpose.

Recently, I took time off from my normal work routine to take in an afternoon matinee of *The Legend of Bagger Vance*. While I thoroughly enjoyed playing hooky from work and the movie in general, there was one line that stood out above all the rest. As I heard the line, I realized it was the main lesson I was there to learn that day.

The caddie, Bagger Vance, said, "God is happiest when his children are at play." I keep that line on my desk lamp so I won't forget. Whenever I'm feeling like my work is drudgery or there's effort involved, I know that, in that moment, I've shifted from expressing my life purpose to something else. Usually the something else is related to some "should" values acquired in the past.

People who live off-purpose lives have bought into the idea of "no pain, no gain." It doesn't have to be that way. Sure, there may be times when you need to exert yourself more diligently, but that doesn't mean you need to suffer while doing it.

I lift weights three times a week as part of my health and fitness routine. Part of the object to lifting increasing amounts of weight is to fatigue the muscles so they will grow and become stronger. This doesn't mean that I need to be suffering while I'm straining. I have the choice to sweat with enjoyment or to sweat while complaining about how hard it is or how unfair it is that I have to be stuck in my gym. I choose to bring joy and fun to my life, and so can you.

Benefit #7 — Integrity

For me, a Life on Purpose is a life of ultimate integrity. It's a life that is whole and complete. People who know and are living true to their purpose know who they are and why they are here. They live true to their core values as they serve themselves and others through the expression of their life purpose.

People who are living off purpose simply haven't found themselves yet. There's nothing wrong with them, there's just something missing. I created the Purpose Process to provide people with a means of putting this important missing ingredient into their lives.

Benefit #8 — Trust and Faith

As people clarify and begin to live true to their life purpose, many of them report a surprising increase in synchronicities and serendipity in their lives. It's as though the Universe is rewarding them for the courage to live true to their purpose. Most of these people also experience a deepening trust and faith. They realize that there is, indeed, a greater force in the Universe, and at the same time realize that they are an integral part of that force, as well.

People living off purpose, are often slow to trust anything they can't see and touch. Coming from fear, trusting looks like a bad idea. They often have plenty of evidence for not trusting, looking back on all of the times they did and ended up hurt. That's why it takes real courage to live on purpose.

Nowhere in this book will I say that a Life on Purpose is risk-free. But I will say, from my own experience and those of the thousands of people I've met who are living on purpose, that the risk is well worth it.

Benefit #9 — Grace

According to the dictionary, grace is "the unmerited divine assistance given man." People living on purpose often report living a grace-filled life. When you commit to living true to your purpose, something amazing begins to happen. The Universe lines up with your intention and commitment. Perhaps W. H. Murray says it best:

> Until one is committed, there is hesitancy, the chance to draw back, always ineffectiveness. Concerning all acts of initiative and creativity there is one elementary truth, the ignorance of which kills countless ideas and splendid plans: That the moment one definitely commits oneself, then providence moves too.
>
> All sorts of things occur to help one that would never otherwise have occurred. A whole stream of events issue from the decision; raising in ones favor all manner of assistance, which no man could have dreamt would have come his way. I have learned a deep respect for one of Goethe's couplets:
>
> *Whatever you can do, or dream you can, begin it; boldness has genius, power and magic in it.*[1]

---

1 *The Scottish Himalaya Expedition*, 1951.

Benefit #10—Flow

All nine of the previous benefits can be summarized within this last one. People living on purpose live in the flow of the universal stream of consciousness. Rather than fighting against the current, they allow what wants to happen to happen. They allow what wants to flow to flow. They know that while they may never completely understand or comprehend God's divine design and plan for this Universe, they can still play an integral part in its realization.

If you don't feel like you're in the flow of life, then you're working hard to resist the flow of the Universe. Many years ago, while attending the University of Georgia College of Veterinary Medicine, some of the other vet students and I took up white water canoeing. Dr. Dawe, a wise and knowledgeable college professor who also loved canoeing, took us under his wing so that we wouldn't drown before we graduated.

His first safety lesson was very simple: When you fall into the water at a set of rapids, be sure to keep your feet out in front of you and your head up out of the water, then relax and enjoy the ride.

What if we approached our lives like this, and instead of resisting, we simply sat back and enjoyed the ride along the rapids of universal flow?

This is why one of Life on Purpose Institute's key purpose operating principles is to "flow with what's flowing, and work on what's working," rather than getting caught up in whatever might not be flowing.

Call to Action Assignment—Part One

Select the top three or four benefits from the previous pages, those that resonate with you most strongly and that you'd most want to experience more of in your life.

Then, take a moment to step into the future—what we'll call the "visionary reality"—where you are now enjoying these benefits. Write a description of what your life looks and feels like in this new visionary reality. As you stand in the future and describe it in rich, sensory detail, your writing will be in the present tense.

For example, if having more fulfillment in your life would be one of the most important benefits, you might write: "In my visionary reality, I'm experiencing joyful fulfillment in my job because I know I'm making a wonderful contribution to others while being paid well for my services." Be sure to focus on what is positive and consistent with your top benefits. In other words, you wouldn't write: "I'm not stuck in the dead end job that I presently have."

Don't be overly concerned about whether you feel such a future is possible for yourself. You should find a balance, though, in which it doesn't feel like a pie-in-the-sky fantasy, either. You need not worry at this point about how to bring this future into reality; simply allow yourself to dream. This initial exercise will sow the seeds for a more expansive visionary reality that you will create soon.

THE TREMENDOUS
LIFE-SHAPING POWER OF VISION

As I've pointed out previously, vision is an integral part of a Life on Purpose. Without vision we can wither on the vine. What is vision? In working as a coach with thousands of people, I've found that vision is a key ingredient of our life purpose. It's what we see to be possible — not only for ourselves, but also for our families, our communities, and indeed for the world. Without it we perish. I've found that helping people reawaken their sense of what's possible is a key component of preparing for the journey along the Purposeful Path. This is because the more someone taps into this realm of possibility, the more inspired they will be to take the actions necessary to make it their reality.

Through the coaching process you will create a clear vision of a new future for yourself, including what this new reality looks and feels like, what you will be doing in it, and what you will no longer be doing because those actions are no longer consistent with who you are. You want to be able to taste, hear, and fully experience this new future.

From the perspective of this new reality, you will look back to your present reality and discover the gap that exists between where you currently are and where you are destined to be. And don't worry, this gap won't be a cause for despair. You are accustomed to looking at your entire life from the perspective of the past and present, forward into the future; but through the visionary reality process, this will be reversed—you will stand in the future, in the visionary reality you've created, and look back to the present. The view from the future is profoundly different. You will know that it's possible to close the gap because you will have already done it! This awareness creates a profound and even life-altering shift in perspective. Here's an example that will illustrate the point.

The View from Mount Everest

Imagine that you are sitting in your living room, leafing through a *National Geographic* magazine, when your eyes fall upon a picture of Mount Everest. You've longed for years to climb this mountain, but in the busyness of life it's been a dream placed on the back burner. Now as you stare at its majestic summit you think, "Wow, wouldn't it be awesome to stand at the top of the tallest mountain in the world?" As you read the article, you begin to speculate about the possibility of climbing it.

What is likely to happen in the process of speculating? If you're like the rest of humanity, you'll dilute the dream with all the reasons why it "can't" be fulfilled: You're not strong enough—you smoke three packs of cigarettes a day, and climbing a flight of stairs is a major challenge. Besides, your family would never support you in pursuing this dream. On top of which you couldn't possibly take off from work for such a massive undertaking.

As you begin to focus on all the reasons you can't accomplish this dream, you begin to attract more and more negative energy—which will probably result in your dropping the magazine on the coffee table, clicking on the television, and lighting another cigarette as you stroll into the kitchen for another beer. *Poof!* So much for your dream of climbing Mount Everest.

Switch Frames to Your Visionary Reality

This time imagine that you're standing on the peak of Mount Everest. Just moments ago you took the last few steps that brought you to the pinnacle of both the mountain and your life. You raise your arms in the air as you gaze over the most majestic view you have ever seen. The sense of satisfaction, fulfillment, and accomplishment is almost more than you can bear. It's so strong that it brings tears of joy to your eyes, and you feel your legs weaken as you fall to your knees in a humble prayer of gratitude for the power that made this moment possible. As you kneel there giving thanks, you take a few moments to reflect back to when the seed of this dream was first planted — that evening in your apartment, when you were leafing through the *National Geographic*. But this time you're looking back on that moment from the pinnacle of Mount Everest with the goal already accomplished.

Can you begin to see how different your perspective would be? You'd be able to see many of the obstacles and roadblocks you had faced and you would know that you had successfully overcome them all. Now imagine doing this for a vision that is a true reflection of your life purpose. How powerful would this be? What effect could it have on your life? What contribution to the world would become possible? That is what is available when we use the power of vision to shape our lives while making a difference for others.

What is your vision for the world? Have you been willing to surrender your life to its fulfillment? If not, what are the obstacles and roadblocks that stand in your way? What would allow you to take the realization of that vision to new heights? What resources do you need to attract to support your vision? What are you waiting for?

Creating the Gap

As I've already mentioned, in determining where you presently are in your life and where you long to be, it's likely you've created a sizable gap for yourself. Congratulations! That's the point to this part of purposefully preparing for this great journey. Between these two points is the Purposeful Path. Don't be overly concerned if the journey looks daunting to you. You have two important travel aids available to you:

- A Map–The Life on Purpose Process outlined in this book, and

- An Experienced Guide–A Life on Purpose Coach

Let's look at this second part a bit closer.

Call to Action Assignment — Part Two

It's now time to create your Life on Purpose visionary reality. This is a living, organic document that you can continue to play with even as you begin to draw this new future to you. In other words, it's not carved in stone. You can add to it, delete from it, and refer to it often. To write it, you'll look back on the following:

- Your Life on Purpose Self-Test–Look at the statements you scored low on as a reference point for what you may want to bring into your new reality.

- Your Wheel of Life–Again, look at the areas of your life that you scored below five. What would these areas look like if they were an eight or higher?

- Your three or four top benefits–Use these as starting points for your visionary reality

Remember these pointers:

- Write your visionary reality in the present tense, as though you're standing in that future and describing what you see and feel.

- Make it multi-sensory and rich in detail. What does this new future smell like? What are some of the tastes of this new future?

- Focus on what's present and positive.

- Have fun!

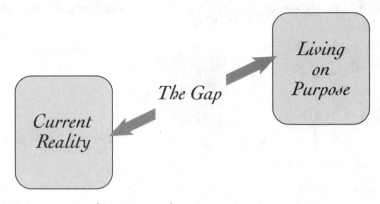

A Visionary Reality Example

Here is an example of a visionary reality I created for what my life on purpose looks like when I'm sixty. While the details are likely different than those you'll envision for yourself, it will give you a good sense of how to begin thinking.

It's so incredible that here I am on my sixtieth birthday and the entire family is in tip-top, excellent health. Amber will soon be graduating from high school with honors and with clarity about who she is and where she is going next in her life. She also has the resources to move forward confidently as she continues to design her Life on Purpose.

Ann and I are thoroughly enjoying being financially free with our passive income streams exceeding our expenses, and with an abundance of discretionary time and money for travel, fun, and relaxation. We have traveled to such places as Bali, Australia, New Zealand, and Hawaii, as well as having taken numerous trips around the USA, thanks in large part to the incredible job Ann has done with her dream business, Purposeful Properties.

Life on Purpose Institute has now been in existence for almost thirteen years. It is a stable, mature, yet still-growing business that has become known as the preeminent place to go for spiritually based coaching and for anyone who wants to bring more purpose, passion, and play to their life. Along the way, we've created and branded our own unique type of coaching, Life on Purpose Coaching. This form of coaching is known around the world as providing a proven, systematic, spiritually based, and practical process by which people can clarify and live true to their Divinely Inspired Life Purpose.

Having learned from our past without being stopped by it, we've attracted a dynamic faculty of passionate and compassionate Life on Purpose Certified Coaches who are the cream of the crop of our graduates. They love Life on Purpose Institute, and are committed to our success. They are also highly effective and successful coaches as well as program leaders.

Our vision has continued to be a World on Purpose, in which people live lives of:

- Purposeful, passionate, and playful service

- Mindful abundance balanced with simplicity, and

- Spiritual serenity

Our "product" is enhancing life through purpose, and Life on Purpose Institute has developed to the point that Ann and I can step away from it for extended periods of time and it continues to run—and run well. We have become more the spokespeople for Life on Purpose, with the daily routine being handled by our support staff and program leaders. Life on Purpose Institute is a well-oiled machine, with systems and support structures maintained by qualified people who are passionate about the World on Purpose we're creating.

A Word About the Value of Personal Coaching

While I've approached this book with my "coaching cap" on and have made every effort to give you an experience of being in a coaching relationship with me, I feel I must point out that the value you will receive from the Life on Purpose Process will be greatly heightened if you work with a personal coach who has been trained to guide people along the Purposeful Path.

Your own personal coach can provide several valuable benefits including:

- *A Structure of Support:* It's easy to stumble off the Purposeful Path when you're reading a book. The sincerest of good intentions can sometimes be waylaid in the midst of life's circumstances. Having the structure of a regular coaching session can make a huge difference in staying true and on course with your commitment to clarify and live true to your purpose.

- *Further Clarity:* A personal coach can act like a mirror, reflecting your thoughts and perspectives back to you, thus bringing more clarity to what you're working on. And with that clarity comes a greater power to create your life.

- *Focus:* Closely akin to clarity is focus. Your coach can help you stay focused on what's most important in your life. During the process, a coach can help you stay on course or return to the Purposeful Path if you do stray.

- *Mastermind Alliance:* Your personal coach can also serve as a mastermind ally, helping you tap into your own inner wisdom. In other words, when two or more gather together with a commonly shared intention, there is a synergistic energy created such that the sum is greater than the parts.

- *A Full Partner in Life:* A personal coach often becomes a full partner in your life, committed to what you're committed to while remaining unattached.

Of course, no one "needs" a coach, and the decision whether or not to work with a coach is a personal one. At the same time, thousands of people are discovering that it makes a lot of sense to have a coach in their corner, especially if they are committed to excelling at life.

If you feel you would benefit from having your own personal Life on Purpose Certified Coach to assist you along the Purposeful Path, I invite you to visit the Life on Purpose Institute website, where you'll find bios and profiles of coaches who have been specially trained to guide people through the Life on Purpose Process. Pick the coach that resonates with you and request a complimentary coaching session to see if working with a coach would support you.

THE BOOMERS AT PASSAGE #1

When Barbara first studied the mental obstacles along the Purposeful Path, she realized that her monkey mind often got in the way of her fully engaging in conversations, especially with Bob and her children. After all, like many women she'd become a master at multi-tasking, which included thinking about a myriad of different things while fulfilling her many duties as a wife and mom. She gave herself an assignment to catch her monkey mind at least once with each of them, then to set those thoughts off to the side and really listen to her family. At the end of the week, she noted in her journal that as a result of the exercise she realized that she not only didn't really know herself, but she didn't fully know her husband or children. While it was an uncomfortable insight to admit, she decided to take further action on it by scheduling in special one-on-one time with each of them at least once per month. It's been a very powerful experience for her.

Bob, on the other hand, realized that he was a classic case of the full cup syndrome. In fact, he finally admitted to Barbara that when she started reading about the mental obstacles, he was listening to her as though he already knew all about what she was going to read…until she read the story about the Zen master. "You really nailed me with that one," he admitted. Bob also realized that he often listens to his staff members in that way, so he committed to spending a week listening for the nuggets of gold that his staff offered to him, which he'd been too full to hear or appreciate before.

The Boomer's Self-Tests

Bob promised Barbara that he would be honest on the self-test, and he was—though he found it to be a painful experience, especially when he got his score back:

Your Score: 58 out of a possible 200.

Your Results: Surviving

Analysis of Results: At this level you're getting by in your life, although many times it may feel like something is missing. Those feelings could be your soul beginning to awaken to the rich possibilities that lie ahead. Trust those feelings and begin to ask your inner guidance system for what's needed to begin fulfilling your life. To do this, you'll need time for quiet reflection. Carving out this time in your life will be richly rewarding, especially if you then follow the suggestions that arise from these moments.

Barbara also answered the self-test honestly and was pleased to learn that she wasn't in survival:

Your Score: 86 out of a possible 200.

Your Results: Striving

Analysis of Results: Your life is moving forward well at this level and you have much to be thankful for, although you may not be fully aware of these blessings. So, a little gratitude work can go a long way in moving you to the next level. Two ideal times to consciously practice gratitude are in the morning, as you first awaken, and at night, as you prepare for sleep. If you haven't already done so, consider starting a gratitude journal, or simply devote five to ten minutes in the morning and evening to counting your blessings. It'll be time well spent.

A couple of nights after Bob finished his self-test, he told his wife, "This feels like important work we're doing. I have to admit that it felt pretty hokey at first, but I guess that was my full cup. Somehow, let's make it a point to carve out some time each week to do this work."

Barbara realized that this sense of partnership was an integral ingredient that had kept them together through the years.

The Boomers' Wheels of Life

Barbara's Wheel:

Area of Life	Working	Satisfied	Average
Family	7	4	5.5
Health	5	4	4.5
Friends & Social	4	4	4
Spiritual	5	3	4
Money & Finance	7	5	6
Fun & Hobbies	3	3	3

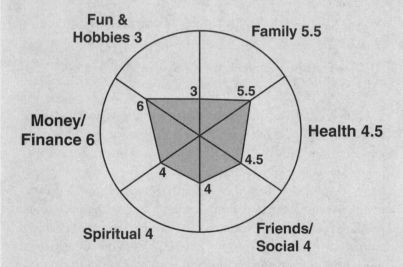

Barbara's Wheel of Life with her results.

When Barbara completed the Wheel of Life she found that her wheel was not only out of balance, but it was small. "It looks like one of those spare tires most cars have in the trunk these days. Just barely large enough to get me to a gas station," she commented to one of her friends.

Comments she made in her journal included:

- While my family is "working" in that no one is in jail, on drugs, or alienated from each other, we're so busy lately that we rarely spend any quality time together. That's why I gave such a low score under unsatisfying.

- My health is okay, but just okay. My energy level is often lower than I think it should be, and through the years I've picked up fifteen to twenty pounds of extra weight that seems to slow me down. I know I'll never be thirty again, but it feels like there's definitely room for improvement here.

- I could almost ask "what friends and social life?" If it weren't for occasionally going to church and reconnecting with friends there, this area would be even lower.

- Our finances are pretty good, although I'd like to see much smaller balances on the credit cards. But even with the finances being okay, I still find myself worrying about what might happen to us if Bob became ill, or something happened to prevent him from working.

- Like with the "friends and social life" area, I hear myself asking "what fun and hobbies?" I used to love to draw and paint, and I could lose myself in a good book. What happened to those fun times? More importantly, how do I get them back?

- All in all, the overall impression I'm left with is that's it's time to reconnect with what I value most, with my family and friends, and with myself. But how?

Bob's Wheel:

Area of Life	Working	Satisfied	Average
Family	7	4	5.5
Health	5	4	4.5
Friends & Social	4	4	4
Spiritual	5	3	4
Money & Finance	7	5	6
Fun & Hobbies	3	3	3

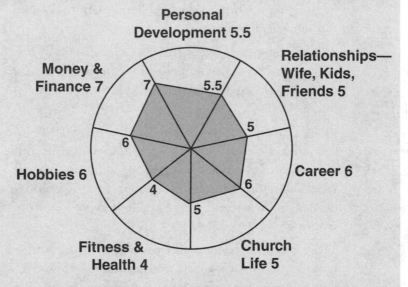

Bob's Wheel of Life with his results.

Bob's comments to Barbara about what he learned from the Wheel of Life exercise went like this:

Well, overall it wasn't bad, though I do feel it's a bit out of balance. The main thing I realized is that while my career is going well and the business is doing okay, I'm finding myself increasingly dissatisfied. It's becoming tougher and tougher to go to work each day. Now don't worry, I'm not ready to chuck the whole thing. It's just an interesting insight. I think I'm at the phase of my life that I want to start doing more things that will bring me a sense of fun and adventure. I feel like I've fallen into a rut, and while I'm not sure how to get out of it, I know it's time to starting looking.

STARTING ON
THE PURPOSEFUL PATH

As you begin your journey along the Purposeful Path it makes sense to choose the one that will get you where you want to go most expediently. To do this we'll start by exploring this basic question:

What is a life purpose?

I'm not asking what your personal purpose is, not yet. In fact, I'd like for us to look beyond your own limited, personal view to see if we can identify a more common, general definition of a life purpose. What would you say the Cultural Perspective is?

One way to think of this would be to imagine that you've decided to conduct a survey by going out on a street corner where you live and asking a few hundred people what a life purpose is. What do you feel the most common answer would be? What would be the central theme of the responses you receive?

The most common response may be similar to your personal response, or it may be different. What we're really trying to get at with this survey is not just what people say a life purpose is, but how they relate to the concept. In other words, look not only at what people say, but also at what their collective actions say. This is important because we often talk about something conceptually, but it may not be reflected in the actions we take or the way we live our lives.

Write down one or more responses that you think people would give if their responses accurately described and reflected how they lived their life. For the moment, disregard those that wouldn't have an answer or wouldn't know what you meant by the question.

_____

_____

_____

_____

_____

_____

Since founding Life on Purpose Institute in 1996, I've had the opportunity to ask this question of not just a couple hundred people, but thousands. Here is the central theme that runs throughout the vast majority of those responses:

"A life purpose is what I'm meant to _do_ while I'm here on earth."

The key here word is "do." Most of us believe that our life purpose is all about what we're here to do. We may say this in various ways—it's what we're here to accomplish, it's something that only we're able to do, it's something we're to do that gives us joy, and so on.

Since we're talking about people's perception of something, of course, this perception is as valid as any other. And as with any perception, it results in a certain way we live our life. What I'm going to suggest next may stretch you a bit, so be ready to simply try this idea on and let's explore it together.

I'm suggesting that when we think of a life purpose as something we do, it heads us in a particular direction right out of the starting gate. It's as if we jump into life and see a sign that says, "This way to your life purpose," and the sign points in the direction of "doing." So when we get to the next question, "What is my life purpose?" we're already heading down the path that's all about doing.

As a result, most of us live a life filled with a lot of doing—and for many of us, a lot of having, which is a natural byproduct of all the doing. But we may be missing something, like the true sense of satisfaction and fulfillment that we really want. It's as if we've taken a detour without realizing it. We wonder how we ended up where we are…but it was that road sign pointing to "doing," way back at the very start.

I have found that when people work from this Cultural Perspective, they often look to two areas of life for purpose and meaning. For many, they look for purpose in their work—their job, career, or profession. For others, they may look in some primary role in life, like being a good parent or spouse, or a "dutiful" son or daughter.

Unfortunately, operating from this perspective has some limitations and pitfalls. For example, what happens if you misidentify your life purpose as your job, career, or profession, and then, for whatever reason, you're not able to continue your work? Some time ago, when I first paid a visit to my local dentist, this struck home in a very powerful way.

As my dentist looked over my record, he noticed that I'd stated my profession as a Life on Purpose Coach. Most people have one of two responses when they learn of my profession. They are either confused by it but too embarrassed to ask, so they say nothing at all, or, as in the case of my dentist, they become curious and ask what it means.

After describing the type of work I do, my dentist replied, "Boy, my dad could sure use you right now." He then went on to tell me that his dad had been a prominent physician in this part of the country for close to forty years, but that recently, due to his health, he could no longer practice medicine. "He feels like he has no purpose or meaning to his life," my dentist went on to say. And that accurately describes what often happens when people misidentify their work as their life purpose.

The same is true for people who think that one of their primary roles is their life purpose. For example, what happens when someone thinks that being a good parent to their children is their life purpose, and then they wake up one day to find that their children have grown up and left home? We even have a name for such a condition: it's called the empty nest syndrome.

Looking from this perspective has another pitfall in that we often misidentify some *part* of our life as our life purpose. But doesn't it make sense that our life purpose should be able to include all of our life—not just our work, not just some significant role, but all of our life and all that we do in our life?

If we're interested in clarifying our true purpose so that we can have a life that is fulfilling and satisfying, we need to operate from a new perspective of what a life purpose is. This way, when we head out into life, we'll be able to travel down a different path—a Purposeful Path that leads to a life of joy, satisfaction, and fulfillment.

Here's a different perspective I'd like for you to try on—the Life on Purpose Perspective

Consider that a life purpose is the *context, vessel, or container into which you pour your life.* Sit with that for a moment before reading on, and then we'll look at this perspective more deeply...

Let's use a visual aid to examine this perspective in more depth. Imagine you have your favorite coffee mug in front of you—or better yet, stop reading for a moment, go get it, and fill it with water. Now, consider that the mug and water visually represent the Life on Purpose Perspective. In other words, the mug represents one part and the water represents the other.

Write down the part of the statement represented by the mug:

_____

And now write down the part of the statement that the water represents:

_____

Now check your answers:

The mug represents the context, vessel or container (i.e. the life purpose).

Your Life

Your Life Purpose

The water represents your life.

Now, let's focus on just the mug and water for a moment. You may find it helpful to actually have a mug filled with water in front of you. If you look at the mug and the water, you can notice that there is a relationship that exists between them. What can you observe about this relationship? If you're not sure where we're going with this, think of it this way: What happened to the water when you first poured it into the cup? Before reading on, see if you can come up with your own answer.

_____
_____
_____

The water took on the form of the inside of the mug, or said a different way, the mug gave shape and form to the water.

Quick Review

In our comparison, what does the cup represent and what does the liquid represent? Choose A, B, or C below.

A. The cup represents how far you can travel, and the water represents the direction.

B. The cup represents one's life purpose, and the liquid represents one's life.

C. The cup represents a vessel, and the liquid represents what's inside it.

The cup represents one's life purpose and the water represents one's life, so B is correct. In this example, the cup is the context that shapes one's life: the life purpose. The water is what is being shaped by the life purpose: your life.

In case you feel like you're about to have a brain strain, pause for a moment. Take a deep breath and let it out. Now, we're going to look a little closer at the notion of a life purpose being the context for one's life. Remember that part of the reason we're looking at this perspective in such depth is because we have an old Cultural Perspective to transcend.

Here are the next questions to consider:

When we talk about our life being shaped by our life purpose, what do we really mean? What makes up a person's life?

To get to the answer, let's go back to our comparison of the mug and the water. We said that the water represents our life. Think back to your ninth grade science class. The simplest unit of water that retains the property of water is a molecule.

If you went any smaller, you'd have atoms—two atoms of hydrogen and one atom of oxygen—but those individual atoms by themselves don't have the properties of water. It takes a molecule composed of two hydrogen atoms and one oxygen atom to give us the properties of water. But what does this have to do with a life purpose? Well, here's the really big question, which will bring us back to what a life purpose is:

What's the simplest unit of a person's life?

What we're looking for is the simplest or most basic unit of a person's life that will retain the properties of the life. When we know this, we'll know what's truly being shaped by our life purpose. When we multiply this molecule enough times, we will have a person's full life.

Hint. Just like a molecule of water has three components, the simplest unit of a person's life has three components as well. Take a stab at it now: What are the three simplest components that make up a person's life?

1. _____

2. _____

3. _____

I learned this, at least, by my experiment: that if one advances confidently in the direction of his dreams, and endeavors to live the life which he had imagined, he will meet with a success unexpected in common hours.

—Henry David Thoreau

THE THREE BASIC COMPONENTS OF LIFE

As we continue this exploration, we'll next identify each of the three basic components that make up a "molecule of life."

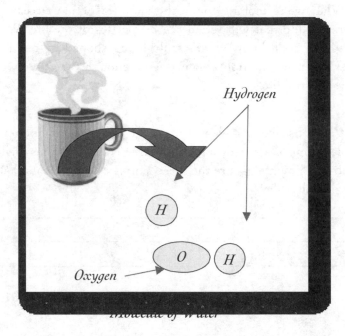

Molecule of Water

For the purpose of this discussion, "life" refers specifically to the period of time that begins at the moment of conception (or birth, whichever you prefer) and ends at the moment of death.

Conception/Birth ◄━━━━━━━ Life ━━━━━━━► Death

Imagine that someone decides to make a movie of your entire life, starting with your birth or conception and ending with your death, after which point the credits start rolling. As you know, a movie is made up of a whole bunch of individual frames. You can think of each individual frame as one of the basic components of the molecule of life. But what exactly does one frame of your movie represent? If you break it down into single "frames," isn't your life a composition of moments in time? You live first this moment, then the next, and the next, and the next... So, one of the basic components of a molecule of life is "moments in time." Write that in one of the circles on the opposite page.

In keeping with the movie analogy, let's look at any frame of your movie. In fact, let's look at each and every frame of the movie of your life—what's the one thing that you consistently see in each frame?

Hint. This one is similar to the question, "Who is buried in Grant's Tomb?" Be careful not to make it more difficult than it is.

Doesn't it make sense that the one thing you'd see in each and every frame of the movie of your life would be you? The second basic component of a molecule of a person's life is the person—a living, conscious human being. So, write "Self" in one of the other circles.

We now have two of the three basic components. Let's go back to the movie one last time and look at a strip of the film from any part of the movie. We could take a strip from the first day you were born, or the first time you went to grade school, or from any part of the movie of your life. If we run it through the movie projector and shine it on a movie screen, what would we see?

Take a moment to ponder this before moving on. Give it your best shot.

Hint. If you suddenly flipped the switch on the movie projector to fast forward, you'd be able to observe what we're talking about more easily.

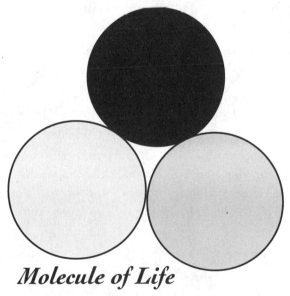

Molecule of Life

Think about it for a moment. Aren't we always doing something? Even when we're sitting around "doing nothing," we're doing something—we're sitting around doing nothing. So, the last basic component of a molecule of life is "Action." Write that in the last circle on the previous page.

Now, let's review what we've come up with and see what this all has to do with living on purpose. First, we've identified that the basic molecule of life is a *living, conscious person, doing something in a moment in time.* This is what is being shaped by the person's life purpose.

You may still wonder, "What does all this have to do with my life purpose?"

Well, you may not have noticed it but we've just made a very important distinction—one that many people fail to make. And in failing to make it, those people are left stuck trying to figure out their life purpose.

Let's go back for a moment and look at both Life on Purpose Perspectives—the Cultural Perspective and the Life on Purpose Perspective. Remember, we said the common theme of the Cultural Perspective is that a life purpose is what we're meant to do while on earth. The Life on Purpose Perspective, however, says something very different. I'm suggesting to you that a life purpose isn't what we do, but *what shapes what we do.*

You see, most people are asking themselves the wrong question when it comes to their life purpose. They're asking, "What is it I'm supposed to do with my life?"

But the doing itself isn't the life purpose. The life purpose is that which shapes and gives context to the doing!

Said another way, your life purpose is the context or overarching meaning you ascribe to life that then shapes the *doingness* of your life. The things we do in life are expressions of our life purpose. They aren't the life purpose itself. The important distinction we've made is:

Life purpose = The context of your life that shapes what you do.

Doing, actions, projects, goals = The ways in which you express your life purpose.

We've all heard the old joke of the man who lost his keys in the dark alley but chose to look for them under the street lamp because the lighting was better. There is a lesson here that can be applied to the way in which many of us go about clarifying our life purpose: Many people are like the man who's trying to take the easy approach even though, in this particular case, the easy approach won't work. They've spent most of their life looking under the street lamp of "doing," trying to find something that's not there. They really need to be looking somewhere else. But where?

Let's go back to the mug and water analogy. The question we really need to ask is what the mug is made of. In other words, what are the key ingredients of a life purpose?

We'll start with the mug. It can be made of glass, ceramic, porcelain, steel, wood, Styrofoam, cardboard, and many other materials. And just like a mug can be composed of many different materials, so can a life purpose. As the Life on Purpose Process came to me from my inner guidance and source of creativity, however, I realized that there were certain qualities that any life purpose should have. A life purpose needs to be:

- *A powerful shaping force in our lives.* It should be powerful enough to shape us as we go through the many moments of our lives, doing whatever we do.

- *Long lasting and enduring.* Wouldn't you want a life purpose that could last a lifetime or beyond? I sure do.

- *Flexible.* It should give us plenty of room to play and to express ourselves fully.

With these three qualities of a life purpose in mind, I asked my inner guidance: "What basic elements will consistently result in a life purpose with these essential qualities—every time and for everyone?" And that's what we'll explore in the next section.

> *Never follow somebody else's path; it doesn't work the same way twice for anyone...the path follows you and rolls up behind you as you walk, forcing the next person to find their own way.*
> —J. Michael Straczynski

THE BASIC ELEMENTS OF AN
EMPOWERING AND ENDURING LIFE PURPOSE

Many elements could contribute to the creation of a powerful, long lasting, and flexible life purpose. In my work with hundreds of individuals and thousands of people in groups, I have found the following three elements to be most effective:

- **Vision:** What is the vision or possibility you see for the world?

- **Values:** What are the core values you stand for and are willing to give your life for?

- **Being:** Who are you? What can people count on from you? Life purpose is more about who you are than what you do. Remember, we're called human beings, not human doings. Many of us have forgotten that.

Let's look at each one of these elements in more depth.

Vision—What's Possible

If you spend much time around young, fully expressed children, you'll notice how they live in possibility. They invent games on the spot and then aren't afraid to change the rules whenever they realize there's a new way to play that will be even more fun.

Children are filled with the spirit of what's possible. Unfortunately, far too many of us have had that spirit stifled by well-meaning people, challenging circumstances, and our own reactions to and interpretations of them.

However, *no matter what has happened to us in the past*, it is possible for all of us to return to that childlike innocence. Not only is it possible, it's necessary if we want to clarify our true purpose in life.

Each of us has a unique sense of what's possible in our own lives—with our families, in our community, in the world. Getting in touch with this vision of what's possible is one of the basic necessities for clarifying your life purpose.

Values—What Matters Most

Clarifying our core values is a refinement process, not all that different from peeling away the layers of an onion.

We often start with a long list of things we've been taught we should value. In fact, I call this first layer the *should values*.

But it's important to peel through this layer until we get to those values we really choose to live in our life. The second layer of the onion is our *chosen values*.

The really important layer is even further within. I'm talking about those select values, usually not more than three to six intangibles, that we'd be willing to give our lives for. These are our *core values*.

Just like we all have a unique vision of what's possible, we also have a unique set of core values that are an integral part of our life purpose.

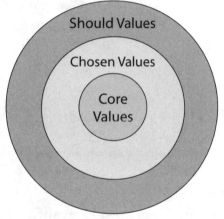

Being—The Essence of Who We Are

One of the most important questions that can shape anyone's life is, "Who am I?" When we can distinguish who we are and the way or ways of being that are at our core, then we have another important basic element for our life purpose.

We all have unique ways of being that we've come to count on and that we know others can count on as well. Distinguishing these gives us yet one more important piece of the puzzle of what our purpose in life is.

The Glue That Holds it All Together

There is actually a fourth component life purpose that is so critical to the formation of a powerful, enduring, and flexible life purpose that you can think of it as the foundation upon which the life purpose stands and the glue that holds it all together.

There are various ways to refer to this last ingredient. One way is to call it love—the universal attractive force of unconditional love that binds us all together and connects us powerfully to the rest of the cosmos. Another way to describe it is your relationship with God, a higher power, or your spirituality.

When we combine this glue with your unique vision of what's possible in the world, your unique set of core values, and your unique qualities of being, we end up with a powerful, empowering, and enduring life purpose that still has ample room for us to play and express ourselves. This life purpose becomes the context that shapes and forms us as we go about doing all the things that make up our life.

From Concept to Reality: An Example

Okay, now let's look at an example that will move us from concept to real life. The example I know the best is my own life. I've enjoyed coaching people for close to two decades, and for the past decade I've also run my own spiritually based enterprise, Life on Purpose Institute. While both of these are important to me, I'm also clear that they are not my life purpose.

I've also been happily married to my wife, Ann, for over fifteen years and I'm the proud father of my daughter, Amber. Both of these roles are very satisfying and fulfilling; yet, they are not my life purpose. My life purpose is to live an inspired and inspiring life of purposeful, passionate, and playful service; a life of mindful abundance balanced with simplicity; and a life of spiritual serenity. Or to give you the shorthand version, my life on purpose is a life of service, simplicity, and spiritual serenity.

This, then, becomes the context, vessel, or container into which I pour my life. It shapes who I am and what I do as a coach, writer, speaker, and founder of Life on Purpose Institute. It also shapes my personal life as a husband, father, and member of my community. In fact, it can shape all of my life, each and every moment of it. Said another way, some of the ways I choose to express my life purpose are as a coach, writer, speaker, founder, husband, and father.

Once you are crystal clear about your true life purpose, it has the power and the possibility to shape *all* of your life—your thoughts and feelings, your decisions and choices, your speaking and actions, and ultimately your results in life. There is tremendous power when all of these factors come together in a congruent way, when your thoughts, feelings, decisions, choices, speaking, and actions are all congruent and in integrity with each other. This is what makes living on purpose both possible and so exhilarating.

Call to Action Assignments

In the game of golf there is a flag at each hole. What's the purpose of the flag? It lets the players know where they want the ball to go. This first assignment will give you a sense of the direction in which we're headed along the Purposeful Path. Remember, you don't have to come up with the definitive answer—simply ponder it for a few days.

Flag Assignment

Here are a few questions to ponder as part of your assignment:

- *Viewing your life purpose from the Life on Purpose Perspective, what is the vision you hold for our world?*

- *What are the core values that you'd give your life to uphold?*

- *Who are you and what can we count on from you?*

Now, blend all of that with the universal attractive force of unconditional love or your relationship with God, a higher power, or your spirituality. Then consider:

- *What context or vessel could shape the rest of your life and all that you do?*

Remember, just ponder it and see what you discover.

In Passage #3 we'll begin to carve away whatever's between you and determining your life purpose. We'll begin with this basic premise: your life is always being shaped by something. There is never a time when it is not being shaped and molded. However, since most people aren't clear what their life purpose is, it's unlikely that your life purpose is what is shaping your life. With that in mind, take some time to work on this next assignment.

This is the next question we'll explore:

- *If your life is always being shaped by something, what shapes your life when you aren't clear what your life purpose is?*

Hint. Look back to your early childhood, the "formative years," to begin to find the answer.

Second Hint. There are many factors that shape a life. We're looking for as many different things as you can come up with.

Go back to the questions and start to identify processes, activities, and practices you do, have done, or could be doing that would help you access the source of your creativity. By that I mean your inner, intuitive guidance system, the aspect of your thinking that people generally identify as "right brain" thinking, your creative spark. After you have developed your list, take a look at the following ideas to see if there are others here you'd like to incorporate.

The assignment is to start doing at least one activity (from your list or from the list below) and incorporate it into your daily routine. Do something on a regular basis that will exercise your creativity and prime your intuition.

Here are a few ideas to get you started:

- Keep a journal of your intuitive experiences and times when you felt most connected and creative.

- Spend time in nature. Practice being awake and aware of your surroundings, noticing the details and subtleties around you.

- Spend quiet time in prayer and/or meditation. Focus on your breath, or the flame of a candle. Notice the thoughts of your monkey mind.

- Be physical. A good workout can be a great way to tap into your intuitive, inner source of creativity.

- Listen to inspiring music and let it carry you away.

- Tap into your creativity through art. Don't be concerned about doing it well or perfectly. Just be sure you're having fun.

A hunch is creativity trying to tell you something.
—Anonymous

THE BOOMERS AT PASSAGE #2

Here are a few of the comments that Barbara wrote in her journal regarding her insights from the Life on Purpose Perspective:

Wow, that's all I can say—Wow! Bob and I continued the life purpose work and today we learned a new way of viewing what a life purpose is. My head and heart are still spinning. I realized today that I've been thinking for decades that my only purpose in life was to be a good wife to Bob and a good mother to my kids. No wonder I've felt in a state of panic these last several months, as my third child rapidly approaches the age when he'll be leaving home and Bob and I appear to grow further apart.

While I still don't know what the "context" of my life is, I feel a sense of hope and excitement at the prospect of discovering it, though also a bit of fear about the whole idea. After all, once I know my life purpose, I won't have any excuse for not living true to it.

Here are some of the thoughts that Bob shared with Barbara after completing Passage #2:

I'm still processing the idea that a person's life purpose isn't all about doing. I've been a great "doer" all my life, since starting my first job when I was fifteen—and in the process I've become a good provider for you and the kids. Now I'm asked to consider that neither my professional career as a dentist nor being a good provider is my life purpose. That's a tough one, I must admit. Still, I don't think it will serve me to be a "full cup" on this one. Besides, as I consider that my life purpose could be the "context, vessel or container into which I pour my life," and that context could then have the power to shape all of my life, I feel a sense of excitement and adventure, and that feels good.

UNCOVERING WHAT
HAS BEEN SHAPING YOUR LIFE

WHAT SHAPES YOUR LIFE
BEFORE YOU KNOW YOUR TRUE PURPOSE?

In the last Passage, I asked you to consider the following basic premise:

Your life is always being shaped by something. There's never a time when it is not being shaped and molded. However, since most people aren't clear what their life purpose is, it's unlikely that that's what is shaping your life.

I then asked you to ponder this question:

If your life is always being shaped by something, what shapes your life when you aren't clear what your life purpose is?

I also suggested that you go back to your formative childhood years to see what influences shaped your life as you were growing up. Ponder this for a while and you will realize that many different factors shape a person's life. Many of them take effect in those early, formative years.

If you haven't answered this question thoroughly in writing yet, take a moment now to do so before proceeding After all, one sign of a coachable player is a willingness to do the assignment thoroughly.

Here are a few memory joggers to get you started:

- Think about your parents and their influence on your life. Also consider the influence of other role models such as older siblings, teachers, relatives, and spiritual or religious figures.

- Where were you born and raised? What country and part of the country we were raised in has a great impact on our life, as well.

- What was the socio-economic level of your family?

- Was your family religious, anti-religious, or agnostic?

- In what era were you born? Certainly, those who were raised during the Great Depression were greatly influenced by it, as were many of us who had parents raised during this challenging time.

With these ideas in mind answer the question:

If your life is always being shaped by something, what shapes your life when you aren't clear what your life purpose is?

_____

_____

_____

_____

_____

Your Inherited Purpose

We could go on making a laundry list of factors that affect and shape our lives, but you get the point. For the most part, our lives have been shaped by things about which we had little or no say. For the purpose of this discussion, we'll call the cumulative effect of these factors your Inherited Purpose.

Now, here's the next piece to consider: just like we each have a unique true purpose in life, we also have a unique Inherited Purpose. But before looking at your particular Inherited Purpose, we'll examine some of the characteristics of an Inherited Purpose that are consistent for everyone.

Your Inherited Purpose:

- Is based in fear, in a need to survive. It's what life fabricates for you so you're able to make it in the world.

- Leaves you with a sense of "Is that all there is to life?" When your Inherited Purpose shapes your life, you're left fundamentally unsatisfied and unfulfilled, although this feeling may be masked by the next characteristic. If the Inherited Purpose had a theme song it might be the Rolling Stones', "I Can't Get No Satisfaction."

- Is a "background phenomenon." In other words, it is so much a part of who you consider yourself to be that it is transparent. Your Inherited Purpose is like water is to a fish. Fish don't think about the fact that they're swimming in water because that's all they've ever known. Fish don't recognize water until you distinguish it for them by taking them out of it. The same is true of your Inherited Purpose.

Because of this background phenomenon, your Inherited Purpose has a tremendous influence on your life. It's like a master puppeteer above the stage of life. You move through life not even realizing that you're a puppet. You're thinking you're completely free to come and go and do as you please; meanwhile, your strings are being pulled by your Inherited Purpose. It's this transparent nature that gives your Inherited Purpose so much shaping power in your life.

- Is a default mechanism. It is what runs the show whenever you are on automatic, or whenever you are unclear about what your true purpose is. Even after you become clear about your true purpose, your Inherited Purpose waits in the wings for the moment when you are not causing life to happen. You never have to worry about waking up some morning and not knowing who you are or what's shaping your life. Your Inherited Purpose will be right there.

One of the most important aspects of the Life on Purpose Process is to unveil what your particular Inherited Purpose is. Here's why: *The more you can bring your Inherited Purpose from the background of your consciousness to the foreground, the less shaping power it has over your life.*

The human mind is like a piñata. When it breaks open, there's a lot of surprises inside. Once you get the piñata perspective, you see that losing your mind can be a peak experience.

—Jane Wagner, from *The Search for Signs of Intelligent Life in the Universe*

PULLING THE CURTAIN
ON THE WIZARD OF YOUR PAST

The movie *The Wizard of Oz* offers another way to view your Inherited Purpose. The Wizard has a tremendous influence on Dorothy and her friends. He sends them all over Oz in search of the witch's broom so that Dorothy can return to Kansas. Eventually, though, the Wizard loses his power over them. Do you remember what happens? Toto, Dorothy's little dog, pulls back the curtain and reveals that there is no Great and Powerful Oz, only a little old man with a bunch of smoke and mirrors.

Like Toto, this next passage of the Life on Purpose Process pulls back the curtain and unveils the forces that have been shaping your life. As you identify your Inherited Purpose you will bring it from the background of your consciousness, where it has been quietly yet powerfully shaping your life, to the foreground. When this happens, you will then begin to have choice about whether to let it continue to shape your life or to allow something else—like your true purpose—to become the primary shaping force.

Just as we all have a unique true purpose in life, we all have a unique Inherited Purpose as well. Uncovering your Inherited Purpose is almost as important as clarifying your true life purpose. If you don't identify it, your Inherited Purpose will continue to run the show quietly in the background—even after you've clarified your true purpose. It can act like a saboteur, foiling your every attempt to live true to your life purpose.

Examining an example of an Inherited Purpose makes it easier to begin to identify your own. The example that follows describes one particular incident in my own life that had a strong influence on my Inherited Purpose. You will not need to come up with the moments of your life that shaped your Inherited Purpose. It is not the moments we are looking for, but the Inherited Purpose itself. But the specifics of my situation help explain what shaped my Inherited Purpose.

A Pivotal Point in My Life

I remember the day very clearly, even though it's been over fifty years since it happened. I was skipping home from the second grade on a beautiful spring day in early May in the small village of Rock, Massachusetts. Part of the reason I was so happy was because it was such a beautiful, crisp day; for in Massachusetts, the first week in May could be spring-like or have three inches of new snow on the ground.

I was also excited because it was only a couple of weeks before my birthday. A week or two after that I'd be out of school, with a whole summer full of beautiful days to play. But as I approached my home, my skipping slowed when I noticed a long line of cars in the drive and along the street. Unusual, I thought. My parents rarely entertained and certainly not on a weekday afternoon.

As I climbed the steps of the wraparound porch, I noticed another unusual thing. Normally, on such a beautiful spring day my mom would have the windows open, airing out the house. But on this day they were all closed and the blinds were drawn. Strange, I thought, as I entered the house through the kitchen then walked into the darkened living room.

I stopped a few feet inside the living room, allowing my eyes to adjust to the change in light. Slowly, I was able to make out the tall shapes of many grownups. It certainly wasn't a party. No one was laughing, not even smiling. It was all very hushed and solemn.

I saw my mom from across the room at the same moment she saw me. As she rushed to me, I thought for the first time that something was wrong. She was crying. It was the first time I'd ever seen her cry. As she approached I felt a knot begin to form in my chest.

When she reached me, she knelt down to my level and gave me a big, rib-crushing hug. After a few seconds, she pulled me back to arm's length, and looking deeply in my eyes, she told me the news:

"It's your dad. He died of a heart attack this morning."

In that moment, my childhood paradise began to crumble. My dad hadn't expected to die at the age of only forty-three, so he'd left us with no appreciable savings and no life insurance. We ended up moving from our beautiful New England home to North Carolina, so my mom could get assistance from her family in raising two rambunctious young boys. We spent the next year living in a small apartment adjacent to my grandmother's home, on the edge of what was considered the poor side of town.

Finally, about a year later, my mom moved us to our own home in Raleigh, North Carolina, but it was only about half as large as the one we'd moved from in Massachusetts. One of my most vivid memories of the many years we spent in that house was of my mom sitting in the living room at a small corner desk—a stack of bills on one side, a checkbook in front of her. It seemed like she spent hours on end in that position, fretting about how to pay too many bills with not enough money.

From the experiences of those early years of struggling my Inherited Purpose became:

I must be smart and have (or pretend to have) all the answers; I must work really hard to make as much money as possible so as I won't be poor and so people won't leave me.

Like most people, I became very good at having my life shaped by my Inherited Purpose. Now, I'm not saying there's anything wrong with being smart, working hard, or making a lot of money. It's only when you have no real choice in these matters, when the puppeteer of your Inherited Purpose is pulling your strings without you even being aware of it, that it becomes restrictive and self-limiting.

In fact, it was this Inherited Purpose that eventually led me to the brink of suicide before I finally realized that life didn't have to be such a struggle.

Perhaps my example may help you realize most or all of your own Inherited Purpose. Or it may still be hiding out in the background of your consciousness.

Sometimes uncovering your Inherited Purpose can feel a little like trying to look at the back of your head without a mirror. Try doing that for just a moment. You know there is a back of your head, and it feels like if you were just able to turn your head fast enough you'd be able to at least catch a glimpse of it. But no matter how fast you snap your head, you can't quite see it.

Like the back of your head, your Inherited Purpose is in the background of your consciousness most of the time. Don't worry. One of your next assignments will assist you in clearly identifying your Inherited Purpose. But first, to give you an idea of some other possibilities, here are some examples of what others have determined their Inherited Purpose to be:

- I must be a good girl no matter what and never get in trouble, or at least never get caught.

- I'll always be a rebellious hippie teenager who's always in trouble and doesn't want to fit in, looking for that "incredible love" to solve the inner turmoil.

- I am always unsure, untrusting, self-doubting, always second-guessing and invalidating myself.

- I must succeed and achieve in all ways, change the world by helping others, stay happy and with my head above water.

You may also find it helpful to talk to people like your parents or your siblings. They can often give you insights into your Inherited Purpose, since it's usually easier for them to "see the back of your head" than it is for you. You might ask them what recurring patterns they've noticed in your life.

To prepare you for the next exercise, ask yourself this question:

What has been shaping your life that is based in fear, a sense of lack or scarcity, and a need to struggle to make it?

Write down your first attempt at what your Inherited Purpose is. We will be working together in the next section to fully bring it from the background to the foreground.

I feel my Inherited Purpose or theme of my life has been:

> *Learn to get in touch with the silence within yourself, and know that everything in this life has purpose. There are no mistakes, no coincidences. All events are blessings given to us to learn from.*
>
> —Elisabeth Kübler-Ross

The Uniqueness of the Inherited Purpose

Since we each have a unique set of experiences in our early, formative years and we ascribe meaning to each thing that happens to us, our Inherited Purpose, which is shaped by these experiences, is also unique. This reality was brought home to me several years ago when one of our Life on Purpose Coaches led a seminar series over several weeks for a group of people in Canada. Attending the series was a set of identical twins—two young ladies who were born of the same parents in almost the same moment in time, and raised together in the same environment. But when they uncovered their Inherited Purpose, they found that they were quite different and unique because of the different meaning they assigned to what happened in their life.

At the same time, as we will explore a little later in this book, there are certain patterns that often show up in a people's Inherited Purposes.

PULLING THE CURTAIN ON THE WIZARD WHO'S BEEN SHAPING YOUR LIFE

> *Our instinctive emotions are those that we have inherited from a much more dangerous world, and contain, therefore, a larger portion of fear than they should.*
>
> —Bertrand Russell

The more you can bring your Inherited Purpose from the background to the foreground, the less power it has to shape your life. As we go through this chapter to distinguish your Inherited Purpose, remember the story *The Wizard of Oz*.

The Wizard intimidated Dorothy and her friends. Desperate to help Dorothy return home to Kansas, they followed the Wizard's orders and ran all over Oz to find the witch's broom. But the Wizard lost his powers over them when Dorothy's little dog, Toto, revealed that the Wizard was really just a little man hiding behind a curtain, using smoke and mirrors to puff up his stature.

This section of the book will act like Toto. You will pull back the curtain on the "wizard" of your past, those unseen and unconscious forces that have been shaping your life.

We'll start by having you watch a movie—the movie of your life.

Step One—Watch the Movie of Your Life

Starting with your earliest memories, begin to watch the movie of your life. Imagine yourself as a movie reviewer sitting in the seats of a darkened movie theater watching *The Life and Times of* _____ *(you)*. Your job at the end of the movie will be to write a review of it. Take a few minutes now to watch the movie of your life in sequence.

Step Two—Create a Lifeline

After you have recounted the major events of the movie of your life, draw a lifeline—the unique storyline of your life. On a clean sheet of paper, draw a straight line down the center of the page. Starting with your earliest memories at the bottom of the page, write down the catalytic or pivotal turning points, large and small, that have shaped your life. Write the high points on the right side of the line and the low points on the left side.

Step Three—Combine the First Two Steps

Now, combine the information you learned in the first two steps to answer the question:

What is the movie's theme?

As you watched your movie and drew your lifeline, what was the theme of your life story? Every movie and every life has a theme: boy meets girl, boy loses girl, boy gets girl back, and so on. What is the theme of your movie? Write down your first draft of this as though you were writing a review.

The Theme of My Movie is:

_____

_____

_____

Step Four — The Qualities of an Inherited Purpose

Let's review the qualities of an Inherited Purpose. An Inherited Purpose:

- Is based in fear, in a need to survive.
- Leaves you asking, "Is that all there is to life?"
- Is a background phenomenon.
- Is a default mechanism.

Now, with these qualities in mind, look again at the theme of your life.

In order to determine what force based in fear, lack, and struggling to survive has been shaping your life, look again at your lifeline, particularly the left side with the low points, and the major challenges of your life. What meaning did you give these things with regard to yourself and life in general? How have these episodes shaped your life? Ponder these questions as you go to the next step.

Step Five—State Your Purpose (Your Inherited Purpose, That Is)

Use the simplest words possible to write a statement or short paragraph about your Inherited Purpose. See if you can write it in the language of a young child, which is what you were when you actually formed it in the first place.

You may want to start your statement in one of these ways:

- *My Inherited Purpose is that I must…*
- *My Inherited Purpose is that I have to…*
- *My Inherited Purpose is that I must not…*

(For example: I must not act too smart or people will think I'm showing off and they won't like me.)

Step Six—Give It a Rest

Put your Inherited Purpose statement away for a little while, up to a week. Just let it rest in your subconscious for a few days.

Step Seven—Polish Your Inherited Purpose

After a few days, take out your Inherited Purpose and review it. Is anything missing? Is there anything you want to add? Does it fit the qualities of an Inherited Purpose: It's based in fear, in a need to survive; it leaves you unsatisfied and unfulfilled; it's transparent, a background phenomenon; it runs the show whenever you're on automatic? If not, rewrite it until it does.

Remember, your Inherited Purpose isn't the truth about who you really are. It's only what has been masquerading as the truth. You've been living a life of mistaken identity.

Often, when people become clear about their Inherited Purpose, they begin to use it to feel bad about themselves and their life. While this is natural, the coaching is to catch this early and to not go down that particular path.

People also often want to know what they can do to either get rid of their Inherited Purpose or to fix it. But the more you resist your Inherited Purpose, the more it persists—and the more it has you rather than you having it. So, instead of trying to get rid or your Inherited Purpose or kill it off, perhaps it's best to embrace it and makes friends with it. Perhaps Arthur Miller said it best in *After the Fall:*

> I think it's a mistake to ever look for hope outside of one's self. One day the house smells of fresh bread, the

next of smoke and blood. One day you faint because the gardener cut his finger off, within a week, you're climbing over corpses of children bombed in a subway. What hope can there be if that is so? I tried to die near the end of the war. The same dream returned each night until I dared not to sleep and grew quite ill.

I dreamed I had a child, and even in the dream I saw it was my life, and it was an idiot, and I ran away. But it always crept onto my lap again, clutched at my clothes. Until I thought, if I could kiss it, whatever in it was my own, perhaps I could sleep. And I bent to its broken face, and it was horrible...but I kissed it. I think one must finally take one's life in one's arms.

What Shape is Your Wheel of Life?

Next, let's go back to the Wheel of Life exercise. What did you learn from this exercise? Take a moment to look at the wheel you drew. Was your wheel in balance or out of balance? If you had your wheel on the front of your automobile, would you be comfortable having your loved ones drive across the country on it?

There's much that can be learned from this exercise if you take the time to look closely. Here's one other thing to consider regarding your Wheel of Life. Its present shape is a reflection of your life being shaped by your Inherited Purpose. When you look at your life from this perspective, what do you see?

The good news is that whatever shape your life is presently in, it can be realigned and reshaped to look like whatever you want it to. We will return to the Wheel of Life later to see how you might want to reshape it.

To prepare yourself for the next leg of our journey, think about yourself today and the fact that you are unclear about your life purpose. Then ponder these questions:

What have been the obstacles, roadblocks, and hindrances to clarifying your life purpose? They may be real or imaginary. Identify as many as you can.

_____

_____

_____

DEEPENING YOUR AWARENESS OF YOUR INHERITED PURPOSE

One of the most unique and powerful parts of the Life on Purpose Process is the Inherited Purpose distinction. The more clearly you are able to uncover it, the more easily it will be to see it in the moment as it begins to shape your life. That is a vitally important moment when you can choose either to let your Inherited Purpose continue to shape your life, or instead to pivot to your true purpose.

As you conduct this important work and become clearer about your Inherited Purpose you will be creating new room for yourself to grow and expand in living your true purpose. In this chapter, we will explore some new avenues that will ultimately lead to a greater sense of yourself—by further identifying who you've mistakenly thought you were.

The "Boxiness" of Your Inherited Purpose

While it is very easy and fairly natural to view your Inherited Purpose as the enemy or to relate to it as something that is bad or wrong, this ultimately does not work too well. As the old saying goes, "What you resist persists," and indeed, that is true of your Inherited Purpose. One of the primary characteristics of your Inherited Purpose is that it places a limit on you, and thus limits the room you have in which to express yourself.

Imagine that your life is like a magnificent symphony ready to be played by a full orchestra of strings, brass, woodwinds, and percussion. But when you're caught up in your Inherited Purpose all you have to express yourself as a one-note piccolo. Your ability to express yourself is boxed in.

In other words, there is an optionless component to the Inherited Purpose. When it is running the show, it looks like it is the only way to be. There is no freedom of choice. Oftentimes, you can capture this quality by beginning your Inherited Purpose statement with something like: *My Inherited Purpose is that I must...or, I have to... or, I'll never...*and so on. Your Inherited Purpose keeps you confined in a very small box with little room to grow.

Fear and the Reaction to the Fear

Let's take a somewhat different cut at the Inherited Purpose and look at its anatomy a bit. Often, a person's Inherited Purpose is made up of two basic parts:

1. There is a deep, underlying fear of something, what can also be described as a "break in belonging."

We're cruising along in the world as a small child, feeling naturally safe, secure, and a part of life. Then, something happens that rocks our world. It maybe one thing that happens or a series of incidents that accumulate. When this happens we suddenly no longer feel safe, secure, or a part of the Universe. Who we are is called into question, and this leads to a failure of being.

For example, shortly after my father died, we were visited by a well-meaning next-door-neighbor. At one point, in an effort to console me, she stooped down to me and said, "Well, you'll just have to be the man of the family now." Such an innocent comment, right? How many times have we heard something like that? But for me, it rocked my world. Me? Be the man of the family? My dad was like a god to me. I had depended upon him and my mom to keep me safe and secure. I couldn't be him. I was too small, and certainly not strong enough. What was I to do?

2. There is the meaning that is formed in reaction to that fear—in reaction to the failure to be. In other words, in an effort to compensate for the failure to be, we "make stuff up." This happens not consciously, but at a more unconscious level—in the background of our awareness. Ask yourself what you decided you had to become and/or do to handle or cope with the fear.

For example, let us look at my Inherited Purpose, which is: I must be smart and have (or pretend to have) all the answers; I must work very hard so I will not be poor and so people will not leave me. "I must be smart and have all the answers, and work very hard" is the reaction to or way of coping with the underlying fear of "being poor and having people leave me." In the years following my father's death I felt abandoned. My father was no longer around and in many ways neither was my mother, who had to work full-time instead of being a stay-at-home mom. On top of that there was a severe financial strain that led to a constant underlying fear of not having enough.

Interestingly enough, identifying the fundamental break in belonging isn't required in order to uncover your Inherited Purpose. Just knowing that there was one is all that's really necessary. Once you've come to terms with the reality of this, look at the larger picture of your early life. Look for the themes or the overall meaning you applied to what happened in your life, especially during times when you felt threatened. Your Inherited Purpose will emerge from there.

Common Inherited Purpose Themes

There are several themes common to people's Inherited Purpose. Some pertain to our relationships. Some common relationship themes are:

- Fear of being abandoned—the ongoing fear that people will leave you all alone: "You'll leave me, I'll be all alone," and so on.
- Fear of lack or deprivation—fear that your needs will not be met: "I will not make it, I'll be poor," and so on.
- Fear of standing up for yourself: "I can never speak up for what I want," or, "I must go along with what the other person wants," and so on.

- Fear of trusting: "People can't be trusted, I'll be betrayed," and so on.

- Fear that you are not lovable: "I am not lovable, No one will love me if…," and so on.

Some common themes about the bigger picture of the world are:

- Fear of being excluded: "I do not belong, I do not fit in," and so on.

- Fear of being vulnerable: "The world is a dangerous place and something terrible is about to happen," and so on.

- Fear of failure: "I feel like a failure, I can't succeed," and so on.

- Fear of being undeserving, also known as the imposter syndrome: "I do not deserve it," or, "If people really knew who I am, they'd know I am a fraud," and so on.

- Fear of needing to be perfect: "I must be perfect, and no matter how hard I try I will not be."

- Entitlement: "Rules do not apply to me because I am special—I am the exception."

With these new points in mind, go back to your Inherited Purpose statement and see if there are any changes to make that will capture its essence more clearly. Also, look for subtle nuances and additional related points that may help you to be more responsible for your Inherited Purpose.

For example, after years of knowing my Inherited Purpose and working to be responsible for it, I recently had a new insight. It came to me while working on a Purpose Project to create a pilot program of the Life on Purpose Process for young people at my daughter's school, during one of the years we elected not to home-school her.

In the process of writing up the announcement that was to be sent to the parents, I decided to drop the "small detail" about it being a pilot program, fearing that this would keep some parents from allowing their children to participate. I just figured I could sneak by on that point.

It was not until later, after talking with one of the parents who requested more information, that I realized that it had been my Inherited Purpose shaping my life, and that a subtle aspect of needing to be smart is being clever and downright sneaky at times. I am now in the process of catching all the places where I am inclined to be clever or sneaky, and to then look at how I can pivot to being of service instead. In the process I am achieving a whole new level of authenticity and integrity.

THE OBSTACLES AND ROADBLOCKS TO CLARIFYING YOUR LIFE PURPOSE

Now we'll look at some of the imaginary roadblocks and obstacles that often keep people from determining and living their life purpose. While we won't examine them all, we will cover enough examples that you can look to see what roadblocks you may have fabricated for yourself.

Roadblocks to knowing your purpose come in all shapes and sizes. For example, if you grew up in a family and culture where the notion of having a life purpose was never discussed, this lack of knowledge would serve as an effective roadblock.

As we've already learned, our perception of our life purpose can also serve as a roadblock, especially if we misidentify our career or our roles in life to be our life purpose.

In this chapter, we'll examine some of the common but less obvious roadblocks to knowing and living your purpose. See which ones you may have encountered.

Where In the World Do You Find a Life Purpose?

Many people spend most if not all of their life scouring the world in search of their life purpose. Despite looking high and low, they can never seem to find it. Yet, they expend a tremendous amount of time and energy in the search. Some people spend almost as much time talking about searching for their life purpose as they do in the actual search. Does this sound like anyone you know?

Being stuck in what I refer to as the endless search mode can take on many different forms. For some people, they search for meaning and purpose in their life through relationships with other people. Not uncommonly, these people have a long line of failed relationships with people who looked like they could complete their life and be their purpose for living, but couldn't.

For others, the endless search mode may mean traveling all over the country or even the world looking for meaning and purpose in where they live. Each time they move to a new location, they wonder, "Is this where I will find true happiness and fulfillment?" And, perhaps, at first the new place offers hope. But before long it becomes no better than the last place they lived or visited.

Others may search endlessly by changing jobs and careers at every turn. These people often have a resume that reads like a Russian novel. When I shared this with one of my clients who had not yet turned thirty, she gasped. "That's me," she said. "My resume is over twelve pages, and I'm so embarrassed by the number of jobs I have had that I haven't included all of them."

Has the endless search mode acted as a roadblock to identifying your life purpose?

A question that often goes unasked is:

What if my life purpose isn't out there in the world waiting to be discovered or unearthed?

Well, if it's not, where is it? That's a question worth pondering a little longer.

"But What If It's the Wrong Life Purpose?"

I've heard this from more than my share of people. They spend a lot of time trying to come up with the "right" life purpose, but they don't ever seem to light on any one for very long. After all, if we only get one life (which I understand is debatable, but that's a topic for another time), wouldn't it be a shame to pick the wrong life purpose?

If there is only one right life purpose for each person, what does that mean there must also be? Answer: a whole lot of wrong life purposes. And wouldn't it be a shame to finally pick a life purpose and live it for most of your life, only to find out at some point it was really not your life purpose but your next-door neighbor's?

I know this may sound silly to you, or it may strike close to home. Either way, consider that a life purpose may not live in the domain of "right and wrong." In other words, maybe there isn't such a thing as a right life purpose or a wrong one. If this is true, searching to be sure you get the right one may be a waste of time and an unnecessary roadblock.

These first two roadblocks often occur together, as people get stuck in the endless search mode by looking for their "right" life purpose. Can you see how this could effectively block someone from identifying their life purpose and living it?

"I've Got To Get My Life Together First"

This is a classic fantasy shared by many people. So many people are waiting for their life to be without problems. You know the ones—they are waiting for their ship to come in so they'll have plenty of money. Then they'll quit their job and live a purposeful life. Or they need to go back to school, get enough degrees, or find that perfect partner. You name it. There's always something that must be handled first.

If you fit into this category, here's some coaching. Consider that whatever is preventing you from determining your life purpose will only get handled once you know your purpose. If you want your life to work, surrender to letting the rest of your life not be about getting your life to work. Paradoxical? Perhaps, but please consider it carefully.

Closely akin to this one is the thought that you've got to handle something about yourself before you can pursue your life purpose. It may be, "I'm not good enough," or, "I'm not old, smart, educated, or rich enough," or, "I'm too old, dumb, poor." None of these are true. They're just all smoke screens we use to keep ourselves small and petty. Everyone can live a life of purpose. Perhaps Martin Luther King said it best:

Everybody can be great because anybody can serve. You don't have to have a college degree to serve. You don't have to make your subject and your verb agree to serve… You don't have to know the second theory of thermodynamics in physics to serve. You only need a heart of grace. A soul generated by love.

"The Person Who Collects The Most Toys Wins" Syndrome

Unfortunately, many people in our Western culture think that they can find meaning and purpose for living in the accumulation of more stuff. An obsession with having is a typical side effect of being misled off the Purposeful Path. Unfortunately, possessions alone do not lead to a satisfying and fulfilling life.

The accumulation of material possessions, which I refer to by the technical term of "stuff," doesn't feed the soul. It doesn't matter how much stuff you accumulate; it won't satisfy your spiritual nature. Stuff is like junk food to the soul, and just as junk food won't nurture your body, neither will accumulating more stuff.

Collecting more and more stuff—or the eternal quest to keep up with the Joneses—can become a vicious circle. When you think that stuff will add meaning and purpose to your life, that notion shapes your life. Life becomes about collecting the most toys. But when the new car doesn't satisfy, you figure what you really need is a new home. So you save and work harder for the new home. But when you finally get it, you find you're still not satisfied. Then you see a commercial on TV with all these happy people sitting on the beaches in the Bahamas, so you figure taking an exotic vacation will lead to happiness. And perhaps for a little while it does, just like junk food will give you a temporary feeling of being full.

But you soon discover that being full isn't the same as being nourished. You also notice that you've maxed out all of your credit cards on the exotic vacation. On and on goes the vicious circle. It doesn't matter how much of the wrong stuff you feed yourself; it won't ever nourish your soul. Doing and having simply are not the key ingredients to a satisfying and fulfilling life.

All this leads us to the next, closely connected obstacle.

"So What's Wrong With Making a Lot of Money?"

Who said anything was wrong with it? In fact, many very wealthy people have led extraordinary lives of contribution and purpose.

What I am suggesting is that making a lot of money for its own sake becomes shallow and unfulfilling after a while. Sadly, several generations of Americans have had to learn this the hard way. On the positive side, many of those same people are awakening to realize that the great American Dream of wealth accumulation is really a nightmare. Thousands, even millions of Americans are downsizing their lives, giving themselves the time and freedom to search for a more meaningful, satisfying way of life.

Several of my "burned out baby boomer" clients have come to Life on Purpose coaching having become very wealthy and financially successful. Unfortunately, many of them have been so focused on their financial success that other areas of their life have become unbalanced. One of these clients, we'll call her Andrea, came to me on a referral. She was a very successful professional woman, making an excellent income, and loved her job—except for one issue: it was devouring her life. At our first session she told me, "Whenever I'm at work I feel guilty that I'm not home with my children, and when I'm at home I feel guilty about the work that's not getting done." On top of this imbalance, she had drifted away from her Christian spiritual roots and wanted to return to them.

There are many other inventive roadblocks people have used to prevent themselves from determining their life purpose. If you don't know what your purpose in life is at this point, accept that some block, even if it's not one of these, has kept you from doing so. Perhaps you say, "But I didn't realize that having a purpose in life was so important until now." That's okay, too, because now you can move forward.

Call to Action Assignments

If we're not going to use the search-and-find mode of determining and clarifying a life purpose, and at the same time we're still saying that getting clear about your life purpose is valuable, then what mode or approach might be used?

Purposeful Sharing

Identify two or three people with whom you can talk honestly. Share with them what you've learned from the life purpose work you've done up to this point. You need not share the same thing each time. Pick one or two different points to share with each person. Avoid just talking in general terms about life purpose, Life Purpose Coaching, or the Life on Purpose Process. While it's fine to do that as well, be sure to authentically share insights, feelings, and questions that going through this process has brought up for you.

A Purposeful Problem

As you begin to clarify your true life purpose, you are also creating a new problem for yourself—it's a good problem, but a problem no less. What is it? By the end of the Life on Purpose Process, you will be crystal clear about what your true life purpose is, and knowing this will create a new problem for you. What new problem are you likely to have once you're clear about your life purpose?

THE BOOMERS AT PASSAGE #3

Barbara Boomer uncovers her Inherited Purpose:

After the inspirational insights that came from Passage #2, Passage #3 was a shocker. In fact, I noticed that I was doing everything I could to avoid doing the assignment, until my coach reminded me that the Inherited Purpose didn't have any interest in my uncovering it and would try all sorts of moves to keep me from doing the work. Then I buckled down.

The movie of my life was quite revealing. I revealed that the underlying theme to my life was that, as a girl, I had to find out what the men in my life expected of me and then do whatever I could to meet those expectations. I can clearly see that this way of thinking stems from observing my mother and father. While they seemed to have a fairly good marriage and they certainly provided for us kids, Dad was clearly the head of the household, and what he said went. While Mom never sat down and told me that my job as a woman was to make my man (and his offspring) happy, that was the message I learned from observing her.

So, my Inherited Purpose, at least so far, is "I have to do whatever someone expect of me if I want to be loved and accepted."

Bob Boomer's Inherited Purpose:

"Real men don't cry." I know that sounds cliché, but it was the water I swam in from earliest memories. My dad was a tough guy. I don't remember ever seeing him cry, or for that matter, show much emotion of any kind other than anger and occasionally rage. In fact, while he was a good provider despite having a limited education, his life was his work and his work was his life. So, it's not surprising that my Inherited Purpose became: "I have to provide for my family no matter what, and I can never show my feelings. If I do, people will think I'm a sissy."

CLARIFYING AND POLISHING YOUR TRUE, DIVINELY INSPIRED PURPOSE

THE BRIDGE TO THE LAND OF PURPOSEFUL PARADOX

Our work thus far has been designed to clear away enough of the blocks, myths, misconceptions, and Inherited Purposes that we can begin the real work—clarifying your "real" life purpose. We'll use the word "real" for now, but we will soon replace it with a more accurate description.

By now it is no doubt clear that what has been shaping your life up to this point isn't the most dynamic or most powerful context possible. Now that we've cleared away some of the debris that has been in the way, how do we go about determining a life purpose? In truth, there are many different ways.

The one I recommend is not the only way to do it, nor is it intended to invalidate any other approach. I recommend this particular method simply because I've found in my own experience and in working with thousands of other people that it gives the most return for the amount of time and effort invested. In other words—*it works!*

The Land of Paradoxes

In preparing for this next phase of the Purpose Process coaching, we are going to create a bridge that will take us out of the Land of our Inherited Purpose and into the Land of Purposeful Paradoxes, the birthplace of your true purpose.

In preparation for this next leg of the journey, there's an aphorism from the Zen tradition that I'd like to share. It goes like this:

At the gate of enlightenment you will find two lions standing guard: One is the lion of Paradox, the other the lion of Confusion.

As we proceed along the Purposeful Path, the degree to which you can allow yourself to be with the paradoxes we run into and the degree to which you can be with the state of confusion will proportionately determine how effective you'll be along this leg of the journey. Said another way, confusion is a fairly normal state of consciousness at this point.

We will also be exploring several conversations on this leg of the journey. We'll start one, take it a certain distance, then put that one on hold, and start another one. Think of each conversation as a thread in an overall tapestry that we're weaving. The intention is that, by the end, it will all come together.

Come together to what? Well, in one sense we're out to address a particular question that came from a previous homework assignment:

If we're not going to use the "endless search" mode to clarify your life purpose, what mode could we use?

I invite you to keep that question present for yourself. Also, while we're out to address that question, we will be laying some important foundational work upon which we can build later as we get into Stage Two of the Process—the living true to your life purpose stage.

Now, let's see if we can find this land on the map. But not just any map—we'll be looking on the...

Map of the Kosmos

I was first introduced to this perspective in the writings of noted philosopher, leading edge thinker, and author Ken Wilber. This information has been adopted from his book *A Theory of Everything*. Wilber's model begins with a matrix that maps the Kosmos, which he defines as the all and everything of the universe, the physical and the non-physical. (See diagram of 4-Quadrant Map of the Kosmos below.)

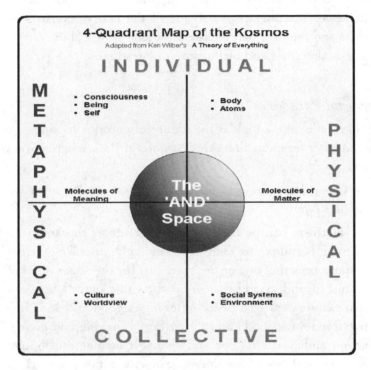

The two quadrants on the right side describe the physical levels of existence, and the two quadrants on the left side describe the metaphysical, or nonphysical, levels. You can further distinguish each quadrant as follows:

- The Upper Right Quadrant represents the physical being of the individual, the physical body, and all the levels that make up the physical body of a person.

- The Lower Right Quadrant represents the physical beyond the individual, such as the Earth, the environment, and social structures.

- The Upper Left Quadrant represents non-physical aspects of an individual, their beingness, consciousness, and self.

- The Lower Left Quadrant represents non-physical aspects, everything other than the individual—our cultures and worldviews.

The right side consists of the components of the physical world and contains the atoms, molecules, cells, organs, and so on that make up both your individual body and the body of the physical universe. The metaphysical side of the matrix consists of the thoughts and feelings that make up the non-physical universe. The left side is also the Land of Purposeful Paradoxes.

Purposeful Paradoxes

Now, let's take a look at the nature of paradoxes, since we are about to enter a region along the Purposeful Path where paradoxes abound.

As Gregg Levoy says in his book *Callings: Finding and Following an Authentic Life:*

> Heroism can be redefined for our age as the ability to tolerate paradox, to embrace seemingly opposing forces without rejecting one or the other just for the sheer relief of it, and to understand that life is the game played between two paradoxical goal posts: Winning is good and so is losing; freedom is good and so is authority; having and giving; action and passivity; sex and celibacy; income and outgo; courage and fear. One doesn't cancel out the other. Both are true.

Paradox is defined as something that appears to contradict itself, two statements that say opposite things, yet both are true. It's a statement that seems to contradict itself, yet forms a Truth.

Here's a thought to consider. If there is such a thing as Truth in the Kosmos, one of the most interesting places to find it is in a paradox because a paradox contains multiple truths. Sometimes, as humans, we tend to see things as either/or, black or white. We are often uncomfortable with two things being true at once. We want things one way or the other.

Here are a few popular paradoxes:

• The more you learn, the less you know.

• The more things change, the more they stay the same

Or my personal favorite, from Charles Dickens:

• "It was the best of times, it was the worst of times."

This statement seems contradictory right? How can something be both?

Your ability to be with paradoxes will determine your level of power and effectiveness, both as you journey through the Land of Purposeful Paradoxes, and as you live your Life on Purpose.

So, lets continue to use Wilber's model to take us into the Land of Purposeful Paradoxes—the birthplace of true purposes. Let's look at the physical side of the Map of the Kosmos first.

What did we all learn in high school science class was the most basic unit of which the physical part of the universe is composed? The answer is atoms. In the physical universe, these atoms form into *molecules of matter*. In other words, everything on the right side of the Map of the Kosmos is composed of atoms that come together to form molecules of matter.

Next question: What's the most basic unit that composes the metaphysical level? Now this can be a bit more challenging because this side of the Kosmos is far less tangible, so please consider this:

The non-physical side of the Kosmos is composed of *thoughts and feelings* that form into *molecules of meaning.*

What I'm suggesting is that the Land of Purposeful Paradoxes is made up of the molecules of meaning that are composed of thoughts and feelings, and it is these thoughts and feelings that give us meaning in our lives.

You may well be saying to yourself: "Okay, I get all that—but what does any of it have to do with determining my life purpose?"

It is on the metaphysical side of the Map of the Kosmos that we will find the answer to the question:

If we aren't going to use the "search-and-find mode" of clarifying a life purpose, what will we use?

We aren't going to find our life purpose in either of the right-hand quadrants—in the physical Kosmos. A person's life purpose isn't composed of molecules of matter, even though many of us spend most of our lifetime looking there. We won't find our life purpose in the physical world or in our physical bodies, because that's not where meaning lives.

A life purpose comes from thoughts and feelings, from the metaphysical part of the Kosmos. A life purpose resides in the Land of Purposeful Paradoxes.

But once again we need to avoid an endless search mode, even on this side of Wilber's map. Just as we won't find our life purpose in the physical world—in the perfect job, place to live, mate, or role in life—we don't want to use the search mode in the Land of Purposeful Paradoxes, either. That part of the universe is just as large and infinite as the physical realm. Remember the question we're out to answer:

If we're not going to use the "endless search mode" to clarify your life purpose, what mode could we use?

Write down your response to this question:

_____

_____

_____

_____

A New Mode for Clarifying Your Life Purpose

Let's go back for the moment to the physical world. Imagine that you are an imaginative entrepreneur. You're interested in satisfying work, but no matter where you look you can't seem to find it. As an imaginative entrepreneur, what are you likely to do?

You'd create the satisfying work, wouldn't you? Now consider that the same is true for a life purpose. Rather than using the search mode, you can *create your life purpose.* And the "building material" you will use is thoughts and feelings, the basic building materials that make up molecules of meaning which you can use to create your Divinely Inspired Life Purpose. You can then allow your entire life to be shaped by this new context, vessel, or container. Once you've done that, you will then be able to express that life purpose in all four quadrants of the Kosmos.

Try this idea on for a few minutes. When you consider this new paradigm—let's call it the creation mode—what do you see and feel about it? When you look at this process from the creation paradigm what comes up?

_____

_____

_____

_____

Inherited Purpose Alert: Sometimes when you think about clarifying your life purpose from the creation mode, your Inherited Purpose can really flare up. It may say to you, "Hey, what do you mean you can create it? Are you crazy?" or, "You, create? You couldn't create your way out of a paper bag."

But none of what your Inherited Purpose tells you is the truth. In actuality, we are all very creative. In fact, we're already creating everything in our life, including our Inherited Purpose. But, there are two ways of creating: unconsciously and consciously.

Now, consider this next piece. It's inherent in the nature of human beings to give meaning to everything. We do it all the time, usually unconsciously. That's how your Inherited Purpose was formed. You unconsciously ascribed meaning to all of your life experiences. It wasn't your experiences themselves, but the meaning you gave to those experiences that became your Inherited Purpose. Then, you mistakenly thought you were your Inherited Purpose—but you're not.

It is time for you to consciously create your life by first creating your life purpose, and then allowing it to purposefully shape your life.

In the next chapter you will learn how to attract the perfect thoughts and feelings that will become the building blocks for your life purpose. You will build your life purpose by discerning those thoughts that are consistent with your desires in life.

The And Space

Before we move on, let's just take a moment to glance at one other interesting part of the Map of the Kosmos: the "And Space." Notice that our map has a circle around the place where all the quadrants come together.

We call this the And Space because it's the place where we no longer look at life from an either/or perspective, but more from a both/and view of the world. Perhaps all of life is a paradox. Dickens says that we separate things out so we can have a beginning point. From the Life on Purpose Perspective we're not interested in dividing life into good/bad, right/wrong, either/or. Living on Purpose is about creating possibilities. This is where we find real freedom.

We will return to the Map of the Kosmos and the And Space later in Stage Two of the Life on Purpose Process, as you begin the process of living true to your life purpose.

EXERCISE: PRIMING YOUR PASSION

We are going to start a fun and engaging process that is at the heart of the Life on Purpose Process: the opportunity to create your life purpose. The life purpose you create will become the vessel or container into which you pour your life, and which will then begin to shape and form your life.

The first step to creating your life purpose is to gather together the supplies and resources you'll need. When you paint a picture, you start with a blank canvas. The next step is to gather up the brushes and paints needed to paint your picture.

But where does the material come from to create a life purpose?

That's one of the paradoxes we'll find in the Land of Purposeful Paradoxes. While you will, in essence, be creating your life purpose from a blank canvas, unencumbered by the limits of your past experience, you'll get the "paint and brushes" from your past. In other words, we will consider and take into account the past without being limited by it.

The next part of the Life on Purpose Process will help you to tap into particular parts of the past when you've been most alive, turned on, excited, creative, and exuberant about living. Revisiting these times will evoke thoughts and feelings. These emotional and mental responses—these molecules of meaning—will serve as the building blocks of your Created Life Purpose.

It's in those times when you have felt most alive that you've been closest to your life purpose. To further expand the paradox, although a life purpose is not about what you do, a good bit of what we'll explore is what you've been doing in those times of your greatest aliveness.

Remember, a life purpose is the context or vessel in which you hold your life. It's this context that then contains our daily lives and shapes and directs our actions—the "doingness" of life. As we learned in a previous chapter, the most powerful life purposes are a compilation of the following elements:

- The vision you hold for what's possible for yourself and the world

- Your core values—what matters most to you

- The essence of your being—who you are and what people can count on from you

For example, for me a Life on Purpose is a life of purposeful, passionate, and playful service, mindful abundance balanced with simplicity, and spiritual serenity. This purpose reaches into my life and shows up in all the actions I choose to take. It's always the same life purpose, same context, yet there are many different ways of expressing it. The point is that *a life purpose is a way of being or a vision that inspires what you do.* Or, said another way, your life purpose is what your soul came here to be and to experience.

Now, don't worry about which part of your Life Purpose Statement reflects your vision, which holds your core values, and which is the essence of who you are. These components are all blended together with the "bonding agent"—the attractive force of Universal Love. It's a little like baking a cake. When you're all done, you can't tell which part of the cake is the flour and which part is the sugar. It doesn't really matter, as long as the cake is delicious. You'll be creating the context for a delicious life.

Your creative mind and your rational mind, and the thoughts and feelings they evoke, will prime your passion pump. They will be the paintbrushes and the colors from which you will create your life purpose.

The next assignment is Priming Your Passion. Before you begin, there are three things you should do to approach this exercise:

- *Ponder your thoughts and feelings* as you live your daily life. As you read the questions that make up the assignment, go through the next few days reflecting upon them. This can be done as you drive to work, take a shower, or start to drift off to sleep. Give yourself a few days of pondering.

- *Write down your thoughts and feelings.* Journal about what you were pondering, and feel free to add anything new that comes up as you write. Collect the data that will become the building material of your Life Purpose Statement.

- *Talk to other people* about your life, your life purpose, and the questions. Other people who know you well and who support what you are up to in your life can be great resources for additional material. Listen to them like you would listen to your coach. In other words, listen for what resonates with you. If it resonates, keep it. If not, leave it. For example, if someone says, "The time I've seen when you were most alive and turned on about life was back in March, when you were preparing your taxes," and tax preparation is one of your least favorite things to do, then simply leave that thought on the shelf.

After talking with people, go back to your journal and add anything new that you've gleaned from these conversations. The idea is to fill your palette with plenty of paint.

Bonus Coaching Tip: Some people enjoy using art to help in this process. Some of the processes my clients have used include scrapbooking, creating a collage, or painting a picture of their Life on Purpose. Be as creative as you're led to be.

Call to Action Assignment: Priming Your Passion

Clarifying your life purpose is a team effort between the rational mind and the intuitive mind. The following exercise is an effective way to combine these two powerful resources to help you move forward along the Purposeful Path.

Working with the following questions engages your rational mind. The memories and thoughts that arise will prime the pump, making it easier to access the intuitive or creative mind. By the end of this exercise you will have a rough draft of a purpose statement. As you go about your daily activities, continue to refine and shape this statement. A life purpose is a living thing. It grows and evolves as you care and nurture it.

Step One

Ask yourself these questions and then write down your responses in a journal, adding whatever comes to you as you write. Ask other people who know and support you how they would answer these questions about you, to bring in other viewpoints. Add whatever new insights come from these conversations to your journal so you will have a rich body of information to draw upon.

1. *What do you love to do?*

Look at times in your life when you were most alive, excited, in love with life. What were you doing during those moments? Who were you with? Ask people who know you when they've noticed you most alive and enthusiastic.

2. *What kind of people do you love to be with?*

Answer this both specifically (as in the specific people you love to be with) and in general (as in the types of people you enjoy).

3. *What are some of the things you could do to give yourself the opportunity to spend more time with these people?*

Think of jobs, volunteer opportunities, sports, and so on.

4. *If money, time, energy, and talent were unlimited, what would you do with your life and who would you be?*

If it's difficult to imagine any of these being unlimited, make a note of this. Then, let go of that concern and continue the exercise.

5. *Who are some people that you greatly admire?*

These may be celebrities, people from history, family members, or friends.

6. *What is it about these people that you admire?*

Is it a way of being, or a set of values, or what they are up to in life? Be as specific as you can.

7. *What values are most important to you?*

It's important to distinguish between the values that you think you should feel are important, and the ones you choose of your own free will.

Step Two

Go back through the material you collected from these questions. Look for the common thread or central theme that runs throughout. Come to it like a detective goes to a crime scene. The detective doesn't wonder if there are clues. He knows there are clues, and his job is to find them. There is a common thread or central theme, and your job is to find it—no matter how well it is disguised. In fact, there are often more than one, so find as many of them as you can.

Process Tip: One way to do this is to go through your notes with different colored markers and circle repetitive words, phrases, or ideas. You may find that you wrote about being outdoors several different times, and other times you wrote about nature. They are probably part of the same thread, but you'll have to judge that for yourself. Remember, if you aren't having fun, you're going down the wrong path.

Coaching Tip: Remember, your life purpose is about who you are as a soul or spiritual being and what you came here to experience. So, as you determine what you have loved about your life, look behind the doing to who you were *being* and what you were *experiencing,* and put that into words that capture the feeling.

For example, you may love to walk in the woods. That's the doing. What do you love about walking in the woods? Who are you present to being as you walk in the woods, and what do you experience? Peace? A closer connection to God? Write those "molecules of meaning" down.

Step Three

You are almost ready to create your purpose statement. There's just one more thing to keep in mind before doing so. And remember, whatever you create today can be changed or erased and rewritten. In other words, *your aren't stuck with any life purpose.* This is very important. All you're doing right now is creating a rough draft to try out for a couple of weeks.

Once you've exercised the rational mind, it's time to call in its tag-team member: your intuitive, creative side. Pick your favorite way to access your intuitive powers. It may be meditating or taking a long walk, run, or drive. Or set an intention to dream your life purpose. Read through your journal material and then access your intuition.

If you're still uncertain about your purpose statement after doing these things, you can find further clarity with the next step.

Step Four

As soon as you've finished Step Three, complete each of the follow statements at least three to five times.

- *A life purpose is* _____
- *The purpose for which I'm here on the planet is* _____
- *For me, a Life on Purpose is a life of* _____
- *The vision I hold for the world is* _____

Write down a brief statement or two to describe what your life purpose is today. Remember, this is your rough draft. It's impossible to get it wrong at this point, because this statement is only the beginning. See if you can keep it to no more than three sentences.

Coaching Tip: Remember, this is intended to be a fun and engaging exercise that will take as long as it will take. There's no need to rush it, and if you find that you aren't having fun, it only means you've strayed off the Purposeful Path a bit. Put it away for a day or so and come back to it. Check around to see if your Inherited Purpose has slipped in to start shaping your life. If so, let go of it before resuming the exercise.

If you are serious about your goals, drop the conditions. Go directly to your goal. Be your goal! Conditions often disguise strategies for escaping accountability. Why not just take charge and create the experience you are looking for?

— Eric Allenbaugh

POLISHING YOUR LIFE PURPOSE

Now it's time to put the final touches on your rough draft. That's right, it's still a rough draft and will continue to be for a while. You'll know when it's time to stop calling it a rough draft and when you're ready to claim it 100% to be your true life purpose. And even then, a life purpose often takes on a life of its own and continues to unfold and evolve.

In this final step, you will match what you have with a set of criteria that will help you hone your purpose to be a powerful context for your life.

Be sure to have the Life Purpose Statement you've selected as your rough draft in front of you as you go through this process. As you read each criterion, see how your Life Purpose Statement matches with it. If there's some portion that is off the mark, then make the necessary correction.

1. **A Life on Purpose is satisfying and fulfilling—it results in a life of no regrets.**

   It is possible to design and live a life with no regrets. As a starting point, imagine you are at the end of your life, lying on your deathbed. All your loved ones are around you in your final moments. One of them asks you, "Tell me, do you have any regrets?" There's a momentary hush as you contemplate the question and your life before you reply, "No, I've lived a life of no regrets."

Now, what kind of life would you have to live to be able to authentically reply in that way? That's a Life on Purpose.

But even more, a Life on Purpose is one lived without expectation. Since that word is used in many different ways and means different things to different people, let's explore this further. Living a life without regrets and without expectation means not only that you are free from the past (regrets), but also that you are free from any attachment to a particular future. This includes being free and unattached to producing results. It is a Purposeful Paradox to remain committed to certain results and outcomes, while at the same time remaining unattached.

How can you be free from the future when you're living on purpose? By being and living true to your life purpose in the moment. In other words, you don't live in hope, thinking, "I hope someday day I'll get to live my life purpose." That would be expecting something in the future and being attached to it. No, you live your life purpose now, in the present, by having it shape you and all of your actions.

Consider, for example, my life purpose, "A Life on Purpose is a life of purposeful, passionate, and playful service, mindful abundance balanced with simplicity, and spiritual serenity." As an expression of this purpose I founded Life on Purpose Institute, which has a number of results and outcomes that I'm committed to. It is what I call a Meta-Purpose Project, which we'll learn more about in a later chapter.

But what happens if, at the end of my life, I've not accomplished all that I've set out to accomplish—all those intended results and outcomes? Will I be filled with regrets? Not if I'm clear that I've lived true to my life purpose and have remained free and unattached to the results in the process. We'll explore this in more depth when we get to the Power Tool for Living on Purpose known as Purposeful Play.

2. **As your life purpose is being expressed, it is inclusive and in service to others.**

When you live true to your life purpose, you express that purpose by being of service to others. The tricky part is to remember to be of service to yourself, too. Your life purpose is inclusive. It's the context or vessel that shapes your life—so it shapes who you are for yourself and for everyone you relate to in your life, directly and indirectly.

For example, if you said your life purpose was to be happy, then it wouldn't fit these criteria because it's only about you. But if you said, "My life purpose is a life of happiness, joy, and self expression, you stand for that possibility in the world as well as in your life.

Again, look at my example, "A Life on Purpose is a life of purposeful, passionate, and playful service, mindful abundance balanced with simplicity, and spiritual serenity." As you can see, it's inclusive in that it doesn't exclude anyone from the possibility of living such a life. In fact, oftentimes, when I first share my life purpose with people, someone will ask, "Can I have your purpose? That says it for me." While I joke with them that my life purpose is copyrighted and they'll have to clarify their own, what I hear in their comment is how inclusive my life purpose is. After all, I'm standing for all people to clarify and live true to their life purpose.

3. **A life purpose is based in love.**

Your Inherited Purpose is based in fear, survival, and a sense of lack or "not enoughness," while your true purpose in life is based in the attractive force of Universal Love, an abundance awareness, and a willingness to flow with what's flowing. This is the "glue" that holds your vision, values, and who you are at the level of your soul together. In fact, it is the attractive force that holds the entire Universe together.

One sign that you're living a life purpose based in love is that you're free of judgment, righteousness, or positionality. For example, as I live true to a life of purposeful, passionate, and playful service, mindful abundance balanced with simplicity, and spiritual serenity, I'm coming from love and open to sharing this possibility with anyone and everyone—without being offended if others decline to share in the possibility.

But if I don't stay mindful and aware, I can slip into an Inherited Purpose position that may lead me to think that there's something wrong with anyone who doesn't know their life purpose, and therefore that my job is to "fix" these "broken" people. And in that moment my life purpose is no longer based in love, but in fear, lack, and a need to struggle. In other words, it's no longer my true, Divinely Inspired Life Purpose. It's been co-opted by my Inherited Purpose.

4. **A life purpose is the context and vessel that holds and shapes your life. It's not the doing of life; it's what shapes the doing.**

    A life purpose is composed of vision, core values, and who you are (being), all held together with the glue of love and your relationship with God, a higher power, or your spirituality. It's not about what you do. It shapes what you do.

    We've already covered this one in quite a bit of depth, but it's still important to be sure that "doingness" doesn't slip into your Life Purpose Statement. Of course, there's a lot you will end up doing to express your purpose, but for now it's important to keep the context of your life distinct from your life itself. Remember the mug and water analogy.

    My life purpose states who I'm committed to being in my life. It is what can shape each moment of my life as I go about doing whatever I do.

    You will find that as you begin living true to your life purpose, it will take on a life of its own. It will evolve and expand. That's as it should be.

    Of course, this brings up another important question. How do you live true to the purpose you've now created? We will begin to address that question with your next assignment.

Call to Action Assignment: Polishing Your Life Purpose

Now that you've compared your draft against these four criteria, use the following framework to polish your purpose statement.

Framework

The framework will serve as the skeleton upon which to build your Created Life Purpose. You may later decide to discard the framework or to continue to use it. Here's the framework we recommend.

A Life on Purpose is _____, _____, and _____. Each blank could be a word or phrase. You may also want to create a short form and a longer form such as:

- **Short Form:** A Life on Purpose is a life of service, simplicity, and spiritual serenity.

- **Longer Form:** A Life on Purpose is a life of purposeful, passionate and playful service, mindful abundance balanced with simplicity, and spiritual serenity.

Here are some other examples of Life Purpose Statements:

- A Life on Purpose is a life of responsibility, passion, honesty, and abundant prosperity. (Notice you don't need to be constrained by the framework. Use it to the degree that it works for you, but don't let it limit you.)

- A Life on Purpose is a life of fulfillment through creative experiences in art, nature, heartfelt communication, and healthy living. It's a life that nourishes the mind and body and quenches the soul.

- A Life on Purpose is a life of truth and freedom through words and action. It is a life dedicated to self-awareness, courage, and creativity.

As you work through this assignment you will be putting the "final" touches on your Created Life Purpose.

Preparation for the Next Step—Living True to Your Purpose

Consider these questions to prepare to make your purpose statement a vibrant part of how you live:

- *What does it take to keep your life purpose alive so that it becomes the context that shapes and forms your life?*

- *Where does a life purpose live?*

Bonus Assignment

Pull out your wheel from the Wheel of Life exercise and make a list of any areas that scored a five or below. If you don't have any that low, then pick the three lowest areas. These are areas of your life that you may want to focus on as you begin the next leg of your journey along the Purposeful Path: how to live true to your life purpose in all areas of your life.

Twenty years from now you will be more disappointed by the things that you didn't do than by the ones you did do. So throw off the bowlines. Sail away from the safe harbor. Catch the trade winds in your sails. Explore. Dream. Discover.

— Mark Twain

THE BOOMERS AT PASSAGE #4

Barbara Boomer's True Life Purpose:

I'm so excited (and yes, a little scared, but mostly excited) to share my Life Purpose Statement. At least, to share it as it stands now, knowing that I can change it and that it can also evolve on its own.

For me a life on purpose is a joyful, caring life filled to overflowing with fun, love, and wisdom.

If feels so good to know that I can continue to be a caring, thoughtful person, and that the real freedom is knowing that I don't have to be, and also that being caring includes taking good care of myself as well as others. I am also embracing the fact that I am a wise person with much to share, especially with young people. That says who I am and also creates a gap for who I can grow to be. Now, how do I live true to this purpose?

Bob Boomer's True Life Purpose:

My life on purpose is an outrageous life of adventure balanced with thoughtful contemplation and contribution.

While going through the Prime Your Passion exercise, so many of the times I remembered feeling most alive and turned on by life involved doing something others might think of as crazy. Over time, I've grown to become one of those critics. I remember how much I loved downhill skiing, scuba diving in caves, skydiving, white water rafting. So, the phrase "outrageous life of adventure" is to remind me of what's possible—not only in participating in such pastimes, but also by bringing that sense of outrageous adventure to my work, sharing it with my family, and bringing it to all of my life. At the same time, I want to balance that by getting back in touch with my true nature through thoughtful contemplation, and from there to continue to offer myself to the world through contribution. I must admit that I'm excited by the idea of such a life.

LEARNING THE TOOLS
FOR LIVING ON PURPOSE

LIVING TRUE TO YOUR
DIVINELY INSPIRED LIFE PURPOSE

You may recall that in the beginning of this book we discussed the formula for growth and development.

Insights + Action = True Growth and Development

Here is why this coaching formula is so important: the Inherited Purpose you uncovered and the Created Life Purpose you clarified in the first stage of the Life on Purpose Process are what I call "meta-insights." In other words, they are some of the most life-enhancing insights you can have. After all, when you uncovered your Inherited Purpose, you identified the major force that has been shaping much of your life. While the Inherited Purpose has done its job of keeping you safe and secure, it has also limited you and often kept you from knowing and expressing your true purpose. When you become clear on what your Created Life Purpose is, you identify what could become the major shaping force in your life. That's big! Except...

They are still only insights. As my first coach often said, "Insights are like a pinch in the buttocks. Interesting for the moment but hardly life altering." Through the Life on Purpose Process you can alter and transform your life. As you make the shift from a life off purpose to a Life on Purpose, you will also be taking part in the transformation from a world off purpose to a world on purpose.

Even a meta-pinch in the buttocks won't be enough to make that kind of difference in your life by itself. We need the action portion of the equation. That's why the second stage of the Life on Purpose Process is so vitally important.

Without this stage, it won't be long before that wonderfully empowering and inspiring Life Purpose Statement you created in the first stage devolves into nothing more than a purposeless platitude. A platitude is "a banal, trite, or stale remark," according to the dictionary. That is just what your Created Life Purpose Statement will become if you do not take action to integrate it into your life so that it becomes the primary force shaping you in all that you do.

The second stage of the Life on Purpose Process is where you will integrate the meta-insights of the first stage and, in the process, transform your life. To do this, we will introduce the Power Tools for Living on Purpose. With these power tools you will have the means to build an awesomely beautiful life—a Life on Purpose.

As we often do in the Life on Purpose Process, we will take the next step along the Purposeful Path by asking you to ponder a question:

Where does a life purpose live?

Think of it this way: Bears live in the woods. Birds live in the trees and in the air. Fish live in the water. So, where does a life purpose live?

Take a few minutes to ponder this and write down your responses before moving on.

_____

_____

_____

_____

WHERE DOES A LIFE PURPOSE LIVE?

I realize that this may seem like a strange question to ask. After all, who says that a life purpose lives anywhere? However, asking apparently strange questions often allows you to access a level of wisdom deeper than what you already know on the surface.

In pondering these types of questions we are not out to get to the "right answer," for there is no one right answer. The idea is to evoke your thoughts to see what arises. Did you find that there were a number of ways to answer the question? Or, once you had an answer, did you quit looking for any others?

I have asked this question of thousands of people. Here are some of the most common responses I have received. See if the response you came up with is among those listed:

- A life purpose lives in my heart.
- A life purpose lives in my actions.
- I think a life purpose lives in my soul.
- I would say that a life purpose lives in my thoughts or in my mind.
- It feels to me that a life purpose lives in my words and actions, and in the results I produce in life.
- I think that a life purpose lives in a cave in the woods along with the bear.

Okay, that last one was a joke. But where does it seem to you that a life purpose lives? Jot down any other responses you might have life purpose in the space below:

_____

_____

_____

_____

Now remember, there is no right or wrong response. In fact, I suggest that you take each response you came up with and to try it on for a few days. For example, let us say your responses were that a life purpose either lives in your heart or in your actions. You might try on the first response and go through your life for a few days to see what you can learn about living on purpose from that perspective. Then, try on your second response and see what you learn from that. Most of the time, when my clients have done this, they've found some interesting insights into what it takes to live on purpose, which is the whole point of the inquiry.

Now, while there is no one right answer, there is a particular response that I'm going to ask you to consider to see what you discover. It is a response that has proven to be a fruitful avenue of exploration for many people, in that it gives them greater access to living true to their Created Life Purpose. Consider this:

A life purpose lives in consciousness or awareness.

Please take a moment to try this on and think from this perspective. In other words, consider this statement to be true. And if it is true, what does it reveal to you about what it will take to design a life that is consistent with your Divinely Inspired Life Purpose?

Take a moment and write down the first three or four thoughts that come to mind. We started by asking the question, "Where does a life purpose live?" We asked this question because we are interested in your being able to live true to your life purpose. You want to be able to go through the day with your Created Life Purpose shaping you in that long chain of moments and what you do in those moments.

I am now suggesting that where a life purpose lives is in consciousness, or if you prefer the word, awareness.

What do you see for yourself when you look from this perspective? How could this perspective assist you in living true to your life purpose? Write your response below:

_____

_____

_____

_____

Now let us look together at this perspective and include the collective wisdom of the thousands of people who have already traveled along this path. A common response to this question is, "Oh, that means that if I want to live true to my life purpose, I need to stay conscious and aware of it. That makes sense, but how do I do that, especially with the hectic schedule I keep...not to mention my Inherited Purpose constantly trying to take over my life?"

Those are all interesting observations. I never said living on purpose was easy, only that it was simple. But let me share some good news to counter-balance the challenge you may be seeing ahead. Most people find that the longer they live on purpose, the easier it becomes. Staying spiritually or metaphysically healthy is a lot like staying physically healthy. Most people find the first few weeks of visiting their local gym to be the most challenging. Certainly, the first few days may be fun and exciting, but that usually doesn't last long. Once the "honeymoon" is over, you still need to do a lot more exercise in order to become fit—and then to stay that way. However, if you purposefully persevere, there comes a point when it becomes a natural part of your life. At that point it is hard to imagine not exercising. Even if you miss a day or two, you don't worry because you know it is a way of life for you now. The same is true for living on purpose.

You can think of the Power Tools for Living on Purpose like your exercise equipment. They are available to help you shape your life into a perfectly sculpted Life on Purpose.

It all starts with continuing to stay alert, conscious, and aware of who you truly are—your Created Life Purpose. We will be exploring the different ways you can do this in future chapters. For now, let us keep looking from this perspective.

If you look closely you will notice that I did not say that a life purpose lives only in your consciousness or awareness. So, what do I mean when I say that *your* life purpose lives beyond just your consciousness? Where else does it need to live?

It must live in the consciousness of others! That's right—ultimately, it must live in the collective consciousness of the Kosmos. Let's not leap too far ahead just yet, though. First let's look at this notion that your life purpose must live not only in your consciousness but also in the consciousness and awareness of others, if you want your life purpose to flourish.

Why? Well, as humans we are relationship-oriented beings. In other words, the space we have in which to be and to express ourselves is directly related to the space others allow us in which to be and to express.

As you read and try this concept on you may become a bit uncomfortable. You may start to realize that we're uncovering a problem. That's right. Remember, at the end of the first stage of the Life on Purpose Process we talked about the "purposeful problem"? Now it is time to more closely examine the purposeful problem you have created for yourself as you have become clear about your true purpose in life.

Take a moment and write down what you think the purposeful problem is:

_____

_____

_____

_____

_____

_____

_____

_____

Now, let's see if your response was anything like this:

People in your life relate to you as they have known you to be in the past. They relate to you in this way because of what has been guiding your life—your Inherited Purpose! And it is easy to see why. You have been relating to yourself as your Inherited Purpose much of the time and have, in the process, "trained" those around you to do the same. That is a problem; but it is a good problem, because once you have identified and accepted it you can go about correcting or transforming it.

You see, since we have considered ourselves to be our Inherited Purpose, we have radiated that purpose to those around us, like the ripples of water flowing to the shore. It's a little bit like going through your life thinking that your name is Robin. Of course, you've introduced yourself to everyone as Robin. But then, suddenly, you find that you're name isn't Robin…it's really Terri. What would you need to do in this case? You'd need to re-educate everyone about what your real name is. It's the same with your life purpose.

The good news is that this same rippling effect can also be used to our advantage. Therefore, while your life purpose must live in your own consciousness, if you truly want it to flourish and grow it is important that it also begins to live in the consciousness of others. The more it does, the easier it becomes to stay on purpose in your life, because people will begin relating to you in this new way.

You may be asking yourself, "Does this mean I have to go around telling everyone my Life Purpose Statement?" No, not really—although it is likely that you will become more and more comfortable sharing your Life Purpose Statement, especially as you learn new ways to share it with others.

In later chapters we will explore ways to share your life purpose with friends, family members, and business colleagues—and even with strangers—without coming across as weird or unnatural.

At the same time, it is worth pondering why it feels strange to share your life purpose with others. What is it about sharing a compilation of your vision of what's possible, your core values, and the essence of who you are with other people?

Before we address these questions, let us take a look at the Power Tools for Living on Purpose, with which you will be able to custom design your own Life on Purpose.

OPENING THE PURPOSEFUL TOOLBOX

The purposeful toolbox contains an ample supply of tools from which to choose. It's likely that over time you will use each and every tool in your box. At the same time, you may find that there are certain tools you use almost daily, and others that you take out only on special occasions. To help you decide what tools will serve you best for different phases of your journey, return to this chapter from time to time. You may find that one of the tools has fallen to the bottom of the box and hasn't been utilized to its fullest.

We'll start by looking at some of the tools that are designed to assist you in keeping your life purpose flourishing in your own consciousness. Then we'll move on to look at one of the most important tools for instilling your life purpose into the consciousness of others. Finally, we'll look at a few miscellaneous tools that can be utilized in various ways.

Here is a brief inventory of what you'll find in your toolbox:

• **Purpose Practices:** Activities in which you engage on a regular basis to keep yourself present and aware of your life purpose.

This first tool is one that I encourage you to use on a daily basis. The more regularly you use it, the more powerfully you will be able to live your Life on Purpose. As the definition says, a purpose practice is an activity in which you engage on a regular basis, preferably at the start of your day, more or less at the same time. This daily practice will increase your awareness and consciousness of your true purpose in life.

• **Purpose Ponderings:** Questions that are posed each day to increase awareness of your life purpose.

A purpose pondering takes a slightly different form than a purpose practice. While most purpose practices will be done once a day, often in the morning or in the evening before going to bed, a purpose pondering can be used throughout the day.

• **Purpose Prayers:** A type of Purpose Practice, Purpose Prayers are longer passages that include your life purpose, and which you say with passion as a created declaration of who you intend to be that day.

We'll also look at how you can create a personalized purpose prayer and incorporate it into your daily purpose practice, if you so choose.

• **Purposeful Pivots:** A Purposeful Pivot is the act of distinguishing when your Inherited Purpose is shaping your life, and then choosing to have your Created Life Purpose shape your life instead.

Once you've distinguished your Inherited Purpose from your Created Life Purpose, it's possible to stay on purpose by pivoting. Whenever you notice your Inherited Purpose beginning to shape your life you can stop the action for the moment, distinguish what is happening, and then begin to pivot to your Created Life Purpose. The more you practice pivoting, the better you'll get; and the earlier you can detect your Inherited Purpose, the easier it will be to pivot.

• **Purpose Places:** Special locations where you go when you need to be restored to your true purpose.

Purpose places are often special places in nature that resonate strongly with you.

• **Purpose Principles:** Rules or codes of conduct that are consistent with your true purpose in life.

We'll also examine the Twenty-Eight Attraction Principles for Living on Purpose as examples of purpose principles, as well as the various ways that you can use purpose principles to stay on purpose in your life.

• **Purpose Projects:** Sets of actions with specific, measurable results that are a natural expression of your life purpose.

Purpose Projects are one of the most powerful tools for expanding your life purpose beyond your own consciousness and into the consciousness of others. As we will see, a purpose project is much more than a goal and very different from other kinds of project you may have tried before. A purpose project must arise from and be a full expression of your true life purpose. While working to fulfill the project you are more alive and aware of your life purpose.

• **Purposeful Play:** Approaching a project, goal, or task with a willingness to play and experiment.

The secret to purposeful play is being committed to a particular result or outcome without attachment. Purposeful play is a way of being that can be especially powerful when you're engaged in a Purpose Project.

• **Purposeful Patience and Persistence:** The process of staying on purpose and balancing the realization that bringing a new level of purposeful living into your life takes time, and at the same time staying persistently in action towards the fulfillment of your Purpose Projects.

• **Life Purpose Coaching:** A collaborative relationship that supports you in clarifying your life purpose and provides a structure for you to live true to your purpose over time.

Having a Life Purpose Coach can take living on purpose to new heights. Not only can a Life Purpose Coach assist you in staying aware of your true purpose, he or she can also provide a powerful structure to help you express your life purpose in the world.

• **Purpose Pod:** A group of like-minded people meeting on a regular basis to assist each other in clarifying and living true to their life purposes.

One of the issues I hear most often from my coaching clients is that they don't have a circle of like-minded people around them. They often feel alienated or alone as they travel their Purposeful Path. However, with today's technology, a purpose pod can include people beyond your immediate geographic area. Purpose pods may meet in person, through teleconferencing, or online through chat-sessions and e-groups.

• **Purpose Partners:** People who know you and relate to you as your Created Life Purpose.

The more purpose partners you have, the easier it is to stay true to your Created Purpose. Sometimes all it takes is one other person with whom you connect deeply to help support you along your path. A partner is especially helpful when the trail gets a little difficult. Purpose partners don't need to be specially trained coaches. They just need to be there for you and know that you're also there for them.

• **Purpose Paradoxes:** The birthplace of your true, Divinely Inspired Life Purpose

As we learned in the chapter called "The Bridge to Creating Purpose," the Land of Purposeful Paradoxes is where your true life purpose comes alive. The more comfortable you can become with purpose paradoxes, the more fully you will be able to live your life purpose.

• **Purpose Pow-Wows:** During a purpose pow-wow you consciously take time in your day to focus on your Created Life Purpose and on what you want to create in your life as an expression of that purpose.

During a purpose pow-wow you align your thoughts, feelings, and emotions to powerfully and energetically attract the resources needed to continue to live and express your purpose. Then you maintain your thoughts and feelings as you take action throughout the day.

• **On-Purpose and Off-Purpose Patterns:** We are all creatures of habits and patterns. Some of our patterns are on purpose—consistent with our Created Life Purpose—and some are off purpose—consistent with our Inherited Purpose.

It is possible and highly recommended to distinguish your off-purpose patterns and begin to release them as you create new on-purpose patterns in your life.

• **Purposeless Platitude:** A banal, trite, or stale version of your purpose statement.

Your Created Life Purpose Statement will turn into a purposeless platitude if you don't keep it fresh, alive, and flourishing in awareness and consciousness. Using your full box of power tools for living on purpose will ensure that your Life Purpose Statement never devolves into a collection of words with no power to shape your life.

Fortifying the Foundation

Before continuing to learn about the Power Tools for Living on Purpose, we'll invest some time in exploring some of the universal laws that have as much of an impact on our lives as the physical laws such as the law of gravity. In our next chapter we'll see how, by following the Laws of Attraction and Purposeful Creating, we can live on purpose with more ease and grace.

THE UNIVERSAL LAWS OF ATTRACTION
AND PURPOSEFUL CREATING

In this chapter we will explore two powerful spiritual laws that lay the foundation for living true to your Created Life Purpose. They are the Universal Law of Attraction and the Law of Purposeful Creating.

First, let's take a moment to examine how these laws are universal in scope by considering the physical laws of nature. We will use the law of gravity as an example. We all know that if we walk off a cliff something will consistently pull us quickly to the earth below. That something is known as gravity. As far as we've been able to determine, the law of gravity is true and consistent throughout the universe in which we live.

Gravity works even if you aren't aware of it as a law. Let's imagine for a moment that we travel to a remote area in the Amazon where no one from the "modern" world has traveled before. Even though the indigenous people may not have a clue what we mean when we talk about gravity or the law of gravity, if one of them walks off a cliff they will fall at exactly the same speed that you or I will. Therefore, the law of gravity is consistent, whether you understand or are aware of the law or not.

In the same way, the law of gravity is true whether you believe in it or not. You may say that you do not believe in gravity, and you may even believe this down to your very soul—but if you walk off the cliff, the same thing will happen to you as to the rest of us who believe in gravity. So, this law of the physical world works irrespective of one's beliefs.

It also doesn't matter whether you like or dislike how gravity works. It works just the same whether you like it, dislike it, love it, or hate it. It has the same effect—this is what makes it a universal law.

Now, I'd like you to consider that just like there are laws that govern the physical part of our experience, there are metaphysical laws that govern the metaphysical aspects, as well. Two of these universal metaphysical laws are the Law of Attraction and the Law of Purposeful Creating.

Law of Attraction

We can define the Law of Attraction most simply as "like attracts like," or as the old saying goes, "birds of a feather flock together." Now let's look at how this applies to the metaphysical realm of the universe, or as Ken Wilber calls it in his book *A Theory of Everything,* the Kosmos. In an earlier chapter, we began to explore the Four Quadrant Map of the Kosmos, adapted from Wilber's work. We will use this map again to explore these Universal Laws and how they operate in regards to your living on purpose.

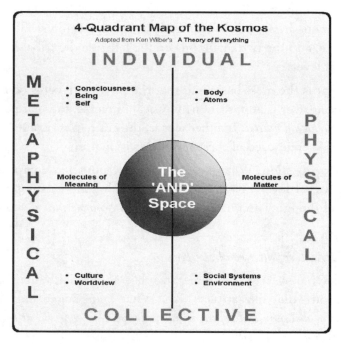

The following information is provided here for your review. If you feel comfortable in your understanding of the Map of the Kosmos, you may skip down to the section called The Attractive Quality of the Kosmos.

- The **Upper Right Quadrant** represents the physical being of the individual: the physical body and all the levels that make up the physical body of a person.

- The **Lower Right Quadrant** represents the physical beyond the individual: the Earth, the environment, social structures, and so on.

- The **Upper Left Quadrant** represents non-physical aspects of an individual: their being-ness, consciousness, and self.

- The **Lower Left Quadrant** represents non-physical aspects: everything other than the individual—our cultures and worldviews.

The main thing to notice in this model of the Kosmos is that it is divided into two main parts, the physical and the metaphysical. The two quadrants on the right side describe the physical levels of existence, and the two quadrants on the left side describe the metaphysical levels.

What is the most basic unit that the physical level is composed of? The answer is atoms. In the physical universe, these atoms form into *molecules of matter*. In other words, the entire physical half of the Kosmos is composed of these molecules of matter.

Next question: What is the most basic unit that composes the metaphysical level? The non-physical side of the Kosmos is composed of thoughts and feelings that form into *molecules of meaning*.

The Attractive Nature of the Kosmos

Okay, now let's see what this has to do with the Law of Attraction—that like attracts like. What I am suggesting here is that *in the metaphysical aspects of our universe, thoughts will attract other thoughts of a similar nature.*

For example, let's say you wake up in the morning and one of your first thoughts is wondering whether you will be able to pay your bills this month. You lie in bed for a bit, thinking about whether you will have enough money to meet your monthly obligations. Well, if you continue holding on to that thought for very long, what happens? That's right. You begin to attract other thoughts of a similar nature, and before you know it you have this growing mental snowball of thoughts becoming larger and larger as it rolls downhill in your mind.

It won't be long before you are having thoughts like, "I never have enough money. Life is just too darn hard. No matter how hard I work I can never get ahead..." Before you know it, you are ready to pull the covers over your head and go back to sleep! That's the Law of Attraction in action.

Luckily, the laws of the universe are nonjudgmental and non-discriminating. We humans are given free choice, which includes the power to choose our thoughts. Now, to you it may not appear that we have that power. Many of us seldom exercise our power to choose our thoughts, so it seems that thoughts just happen. While sometimes thoughts do just appear, we always have the final say as to which thoughts we hold onto with our attention and intention, and which we gently let go.

As a Zen master once said, "Thoughts are like birds in flight. We may not have much control over them flying over our head, but we can keep them from nesting in our hair."

In other words, we may also choose to wake up in the morning thinking thoughts of gratitude and appreciation. And if we do, by the Law of Attraction, we will begin to attract other thoughts of a similar nature. Once again we will begin a snowball of thoughts, only this time ones of gratitude and appreciation.

You may be thinking, "So what? What's the big deal about our thoughts?" Well, consider this: everything that exists in the physical universe that is made by humankind first arose from the metaphysical side, and first existed as an idea—also known as a thought. Our thoughts have tremendous creative potential.

For example, I didn't just start writing this book. First, the idea to write it formed in my mind. Of course, lots of people have the idea to write a book someday. Some of them act upon those thoughts, and many of them don't. So, how do we build a bridge from the metaphysical realm of the universe into the physical? How do we turn our thoughts, dreams, and visions into physical reality? That's where the second universal law—the Law of Purposeful Creating—comes into play.

Law of Purposeful Creating

The Law of Attraction and the Law of Purposeful Creating operate so closely together that it is difficult to talk about one without introducing the other. Let's use another metaphor to expand our awareness of these powerful universal laws.

I'm sure that you are familiar with the attractive properties of a magnet, even if you don't remember how one works. Magnets are composed of a piece of iron that has a magnetic force field around it. If another small piece of iron, like an iron filing, comes within the range of the force field, it will be attracted to the magnet.

Consider for a moment that we are like magnets. The only real difference is that the force field around us is composed of our thoughts. The more powerful the thoughts you have, the stronger the attractive property of the force field.

Now, there is another kind of magnet that is much more powerful than the regular old piece of iron we just described: it is called an electromagnet. We can make an electromagnet by wrapping wire around a piece of iron and then passing an electrical charge through the wire. Electromagnets can be made so powerful that they can easily pick up an automobile. They have that much attractive power.

Let's say we wanted to turn ourselves into a powerful electromagnet. How would we go about turning our thoughts into such a powerful force field? What would be the equivalent of the electrical field for us human magnets? Take a moment to ponder these questions before continuing, and then write down your response.

_____

_____

_____

_____

If you wrote "feelings" or "emotions," you are right. Our feelings can powerfully supercharge our thoughts to attract similar thoughts and other forms of resources to us. Let's go back to our earlier example.

You are lying in bed worrying about whether you will be able to pay your bills. Worry is simply a way we describe thoughts about something we don't want in our life. But are you just lying there having those thoughts? Probably not—if you were just having the thoughts by themselves, you would not be attracting nearly as much. Most of the time, such thoughts are accompanied by powerful emotions such as fear, scarcity, anger, anxiety, and frustration. *Notice that these thoughts and feelings are consistent with the Inherited Purpose.*

However, if you are lying in bed having thoughts of gratitude and appreciation, then you can supercharge these thoughts with feelings of love, abundance, and joy. In those moments your Created Life Purpose is shaping your life. In fact, a very powerful way to start your day is to lie in bed thinking and feeling your Created Life Purpose Statement. In doing this, you start your day by allowing your Created Life Purpose to shape your life.

In other words, your thoughts and feelings act as a powerful tag team to attract the resources that make up your life. And this is how the metaphysical part of the Kosmos is related to the physical part. The bridge that connects the metaphysical to the physical is composed of two primary building blocks:

- What you say: what you declare to be possible, what you promise, what you request, and so on.
- What you do: the actions that are consistent with what you say.

Now, here's a most important point: *The more you align your thoughts, feelings, words, and actions, the more congruent your creative energies will be—resulting in an increased ease and flow of the creative process.*

One significant challenge that many people experience is that these tools for creating—our thoughts, feelings, words, and actions—aren't aligned. We may say one thing while thinking and feeling another, and then take actions that come from some mixture of it all. The result is a bit like trying to drive your car with one foot on the accelerator while the other foot is on the brake. It is pretty tough on the old engine.

The And Space

Now let's look more closely at the And Space—the space right in the center of the map, where all the quadrants come together. In this space we no longer need to look for or live from an *either/or* perspective. Neither do we need to come to life from a good/bad or right/wrong view of the world. It's in living from the And Space that we find real freedom.

Let's look at an example of the And Space. We've already considered where a body lives and where a thought lives, but what about music? Where would you say music lives?

Think back to the time when the United States Men's Gymnastics team won its first team medal since the 1984 Los Angeles Olympics. Imagine you are gathered around the television set with your family, and your son or daughter or grandchild dreams of being an Olympian someday. They begin to play the Star Spangled Banner…

Where does *that* musical experience live? Does it live in only the physical side of the Kosmos? Does it live only on the nonphysical side? No, it lives on both sides, and in all four quadrants. It lives in the And Space—not *either* in the metaphysical or in the physical…not *either* the corporate *or* the individual. It lives in *all four*.

And this is where your life purpose can live, breathe, grow, and be nurtured most ably. We can use the energy of all the quadrants to energize and enhance life. Said another way, *your life purpose arises from the metaphysical and is expressed throughout all the four quadrants of the Kosmos.*

The Law of Attraction
and the Inherited Purpose in Couples

From time to time I find myself coaching couples to live their lives on purpose. One thing I've noticed is how two people's Inherited Purposes can play off of each other, and in the process create a vicious, downward-spiraling circle that can result in some very big arguments. It often goes like this:

One person says something that the other person feels threatened by. "Honey, I'm thinking of buying a yacht." Honey's lack-based Inherited Purpose of never having enough money is inflamed.

Honey responds with, "But, Sweetie, can we really afford it? After all, it won't be long before Alice will be going off to college," which inflames Sweetie's Inherited Purpose of never being able to get his way.

"But Honey, Alice won't be going away to college for another four years, and besides, think of how much fun we could all have together with our own boat. I've already found the perfect boat for us, and have already put down a deposit on it. Trust me on this one. I know what I'm doing."

Of course, a part of Honey's Inherited Purpose is that men can never really be trusted, so this last comment has the opposite effect that her husband had hoped for. Unless and until one or the other parties recognizes the dynamics of this vicious circle, it will continue in its downward spiral. But as we will learn shortly, there is a powerful tool for living on purpose, called the Purposeful Pivot, which can be used to change the direction of this spiraling effect.

The Sea of Meaning in Which We Live

There is an old saying that goes something like this: "Man is to himself as water is to a fish." I'd like to paraphrase and expand that statement just a bit and ask you to consider this:

People are born into and live in a "Sea of Meaning," which has as much impact on our lives as water does on the life of a fish—and is just as transparent and outside our awareness most of the time.

The "Sea of Meaning" is a metaphor for how the nonphysical part of the Kosmos affects our experience of life in the physical world in which we live. Now, let's weave this way of looking at life together with another distinction, known as the Be–Do–Have Model.

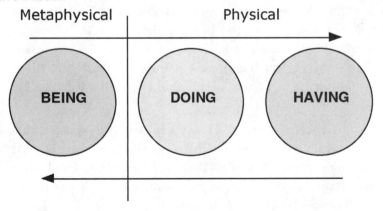

Consider each of the three circles to be different aspects of a person's life. We all have a part of our life that can be labeled as "having." For example, most of us have jobs, homes, people we care about, material "stuff," and so on. Then there's the aspect of our life called "doing." As we explored in the very beginning of the Life on Purpose Process, we are always doing something in each moment of time that makes up our lives. Finally, there's the part of life called "being." Just like we're doing something in each moment of our life, we're also always being something in each moment. In truth, it is often a mixture of different "ways of being."

Yet, while the arenas of doing and having have received a lot of attention in our society, the domain of being has received considerably less attention. This is in part because it is much easier to be aware and awake to the physical part of the Kosmos, which is made up of having and doing.

What I am suggesting is that the real power to shape and form our experience of the physical world lies in the domain of being, and that it is this metaphysical domain that is composed of molecules of meaning that arise from the combining of our thoughts and feelings.

Now, I am going to ask you to try something on that may at first not appear to fit; but I believe if you stay with the exploration, it will reveal something quite enlightening and enlivening. First, I am going to suggest that most of us live our lives in the wrong direction, or at least the direction that is least powerful and effective.

Conventionally, we approach life from the having and doing domains, rather than from the being domain, as the lower arrow in the diagram indicates. But true power can only arise in reversing this order, because it is in this direction that the universe flows.

Who we are being, including who we consider ourselves to be, always informs or determines what actions we see to take, including the actions of what we say—our communication. But what is it that makes up who we consider ourselves to be? Our being nature is made up of our thoughts and feelings. Therefore, it is the sum total of our thoughts, feelings, words, and actions that determines what we have in our lives.

The real question then is, "From where do our thoughts and feelings arise?" The answer from the Life on Purpose Perspective is that they arise from one of two places: either from our Created Life Purpose or from our Inherited Purpose.

Here is another way of asking the question that we have been exploring along this Purposeful Path:

In this moment, what is shaping your life—your Universal Love-based Created Life Purpose, or your fear-based Inherited Purpose?

THREE DIFFERENT APPROACHES
TO BUILDING A LIFE ON PURPOSE

There are at least three different approaches to building a Life on Purpose, as listed below. In truth, many people may use some combination of these:

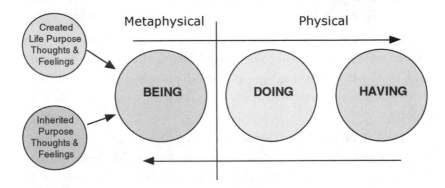

The Dynamite Approach

Some people become so excited when they finally clarify their true life purpose or are so frustrated by the way their life has been that they're tempted to "dynamite" their old life altogether. In extreme cases, they are ready to quit their job (even if they have no savings or reserves), divorce their spouse, and buy a ticket to India, where they plan to sit on the side of a mountain and meditate.

Of course, dynamiting your life can have some interesting side effects, which you may not be prepared to deal with. At the same time, you may have done such a job on your life that the best thing really would be for you to dynamite it. That's for you to say. My job as your coach is to simply point out the different ways to approach re-shaping your life so that you can make an informed decision, and to encourage you to consider the side effects that the dynamite approach is likely to have on you and those around you.

For example, several years ago I coached a woman from the Midwest to clarify her life purpose. She was a great client, very open to the possibility she saw for herself and for her husband of about twenty-two years. Unfortunately, he couldn't or wouldn't see the possibility of making any of the changes in their life. It wasn't that he was all that content with their life together, but that he was resigned to it. So, after months of trying to enroll him into a new possibility for their lives, she finally decided to follow the bread-crumbs of her passion with or without him.

She traveled with her daughter to Hawaii and fell in love with its ambience. During the trip she realized that this was where she wanted to live and to set up her own healing center. But upon returning to the Midwest she couldn't get her husband to even consider the idea. He was stuck in playing it safe and secure, even though he readily admitted to being unhappy in their present situation. The long and the short of it was that she eventually divorced her husband and moved to Hawaii to start her retreat center.

It was a challenging coaching relationship for me, since I heartily believe in and support the sanctity of marriage and the marriage vows. I also had to work through my own Inherited Purpose issues, wondering if I might get a phone call or visit from the irate husband accusing me of brainwashing his wife and turning her against him.

The Hammer and Chisel Approach

For many people, it seems more logical and sound to re-shape their life on purpose using the hammer and chisel approach, which involves mindfully chiseling off aspects of life that no longer feel like they are a fit. This approach is a little bit like how Michelangelo was reported to have carved his famous stature of David: he saw David in the block of marble, and then carved away anything that wasn't David.

Examples of this approach might include:

- Making certain changes in your work situation over time

- Letting certain friendships that were based in your Inherited Purpose drift away

- Suggesting changes that could be made so that your relationship with your spouse could be more in line with your Life on Purpose

- Dropping activities that have come from your Inherited Purpose and replacing them with activities that are in alignment with your true purpose

What are some ways you could see using a hammer and chisel to carve out your artistic masterpiece?

_____

_____

_____

_____

The Polishing Cloth Approach

The final approach is the subtlest of all. This is where you gently polish your life to be a reflection of your true purpose by bringing your life purpose to bear in each moment. This can also include using certain of the Power Tools for Living on Purpose, such as the Purpose Practice and Ponderings, which we'll discuss in more detail as we begin to look more closely at the various tools available for living on purpose.

Whichever of these approaches you choose to use, remember that the primary intention is not change for change's sake, but change that will bring more of your life into alignment with your vision for what's possible, your core values, and the essence of who you are. In this way, you will find that you don't have to wait for someday to come before you're living on purpose; you can begin to experience it right now. In fact, *right* now is really the only time you can ever experience living on purpose.

Now, let's explore the Power Tools for Living on Purpose that will help you consciously create a life that works in harmony with the Universal Law of Attraction and Purposeful Creating. We'll start with Purpose Practices, Ponderings, and Prayers.

PURPOSEFUL PRACTICES, PONDERINGS, AND PRAYERS

Now let's take a more in-depth look at one of the most important and often used tools—the Purpose Practice. At the same time we will get better acquainted with Purpose Ponderings, and Purpose Prayers.

Purpose Practice

A Purpose Practice is an activity in which you engage on a regular basis to keep yourself present and aware of your life purpose. You can think of a Purpose Practice much like a spiritual practice. Many people have regular spiritual practices that help them to stay aware of their relationship with God or a higher power. Some examples of a spiritual practice include:

- Reading spiritual material each day
- Saying a blessing before meals
- Attending a spiritual service once or more each week
- Saying a prayer as you drift off to sleep
- Meditating regularly

Let's look at one of these in a bit more depth. Many people say a blessing before each meal, with the intention of being more aware of the bountiful resources they receive from God. But what often happens to these daily blessings? For many people this spiritual practice often devolves into habit. What's the difference between a practice and a habit? They are both something you do on a regular basis over time. However, a habit is usually done automatically without increasing your awareness of anything, while a practice increases your awareness.

Of course, there are good habits and there are bad habits. I have the habit of brushing my teeth each morning, and while I consider that a good habit, it doesn't really raise my consciousness about anything. In fact, it is not unusual for me to not remember whether I've brushed my teeth—it's done that automatically.

A classic example of a blessing that is often recited automatically would be:

Good food, good meat, good God, let's eat.

When we say a blessing automatically in this way, it does little or nothing to increase our awareness of God or the abundance all around us. The same can happen with a Purpose Practice. In the beginning, it may be very inspiring to you, and that's what you want. Yet over days, weeks, and months it is important to stay vigilant so that the practice doesn't devolve into a habit. Here is another Purposeful Paradox: while it is a good idea to develop the habit of a daily Purpose Practice, you do not want the practice itself to become something you do automatically, without being mindful and aware.

As we will learn in the exercise at the end of this chapter, Creating Powerful Purpose Practices and Ponderings, it is important that your Purpose Practice be something that fits naturally into your daily routine. If it is too difficult to do, most people simply won't maintain it on a regular basis. Remember, you want to develop a habit of doing your Purpose Practice each day without letting the actual practicing of it devolve into a mindless exercise.

Here are some examples of powerful Purpose Practices others have created:

- One of my clients, a very successful real estate investor, loves long-distance running. Since he runs five to six times per week, he decided to incorporate his Purpose Practice into his running regimen. Each time he runs he waits until he gets into the "running zone," then he begins to recite his Life Purpose Statement to himself, often out loud. He says it not only keeps his life purpose alive and well, but also enhances his running experience.

- Another client loves to sing in the shower. Since showering is a part of her daily routine, she created a song out of her Life Purpose Statement—so she can sing about her life purpose as she showers.

- A third client has a small dog who needs to be walked at least three times each day. She uses her time exercising her dog to also recite and to ponder her life purpose not just once a day, but three times.

Now, let's look at another kind of Purpose Practice that you can incorporate throughout your day to stay on purpose.

Purpose Ponderings

A Purpose Pondering is a question that is posed each day to increase awareness of your life purpose. It is actually a modified Purpose Practice. Unlike most Purpose Practices, which are done only once a day, either at the start of the day or at the end, a Purpose Pondering is a question that can be pondered throughout the day. Starting your day with a Purpose Practice and then supplementing it throughout the day with a Purpose Pondering makes a powerful combination.

Here are a few examples of Purpose Ponderings that are based on my own life purpose that my Life on Purpose is a purposeful, passionate, and playful life of service, mindful abundance balanced with simplicity, and spiritual serenity:

- In this moment, am I living a life of service, simplicity, and spiritual serenity?
- In this moment, how can I be of service in a simple and serene manner?
- In this moment, am I living a purposeful, passionate, and playful life of service?

In some Zen monasteries they sound a gong randomly throughout the day. Upon hearing the sound, the monks stop for just a moment to become present and mindful to their surroundings. You can use your Purpose Ponderings like a gong, allowing you to interrupt the automatic nature of your Inherited Purpose.

Lastly, let's look at a way to use an expanded form of your Life Purpose Statement to empower you throughout your day.

Purpose Prayer

A type of Purpose Practice, a Purpose Prayer is a longer passage that includes your life purpose, and which you say with passion as a created declaration of who you intend to be that day.

One of my favorite Purpose Practices is my morning walk. Since I live in a particularly beautiful part of the world—the Blue Ridge Mountains of North Carolina—I find that walking in nature allows me to easily get in touch with my life purpose and the Divine Energy from which it comes. Often on my walks I recite the following Purpose Prayer out loud.

Good morning Mother-Father God, Infinite Universe, I come in this moment to co-create who I am—and who I am is who I say I am into your generous, gentle, grace-filled, and loving listening. Who I say I am is a divine spiritual being choosing to live *an inspired and inspiring life of purposeful, passionate, and playful service; a life of mindful abundance balanced with simplicity, and spiritual serenity.* This is who I am.

I rest in the assurance of knowing and trusting down to the very core of my being and soul that as I live true to this purpose I have said myself to be, the entire Universe/God continues to provide amply, abundantly, and in perfect timing all the resources necessary for the ongoing expression and fulfillment of this purpose.

Therefore, my job first and foremost is to continue living true to this purpose, and I do. I live a purposeful, passionate, and playful life of service, a life of mindful abundance balanced with simplicity, and a life of spiritual serenity. It is this clarity of purpose that I am so grateful for, because it allows me to tap into a wellspring of passion, enthusiasm, love, and wisdom as I purposefully, passionately, and playfully—in awe and wonder, free and flowing—be of service to all of humankind, to life itself, to dear, sweet Mother Earth, and ultimately to God.

I also live a life of mindful abundance balanced with simplicity, in that I know and experience living in and being an integral part of an infinitely abundant universe, where there are ample resources of every form and description readily available for the asking. I balance this deep knowing with a simple and elegant way of life.

Most importantly of all, I live a life of spiritual serenity, knowing that I am consistently connected to and in communication with the cosmic consciousness and creator of this incredible Kosmos, whom I know as God.

Of course, a purposeful prayer doesn't have to be this long to be very effective. Here are a couple of shorter ones. The first is what Suzanne Wade of Seaford, Delaware uses each morning to remind herself that her life purpose is a life of joyful, passionate, creative fulfillment and abundance in tune with nature, wisdom, and service to others.

I am now beginning a new day. God, please help me to bring joy, passion, and creativity to all I come in contact with and to all that I do. Help me to appreciate all that I may learn from others and to see how this day will enhance my life and the lives of those around me. Keep me mindful of the beauty and abundance of the natural world You have created. Above all, help me to make the most of this time You have graciously given me.

The second is from Jeff McFarland of Columbia, Maryland, whose life purpose is an audacious and spiritually awakened life of abundant wisdom and creativity, love and compassion, peace and joy, as well as of inspirational service to others.

I am a dynamic expression of the infinite—whole and complete. Centered in God, my life experience flows with ease and grace—free of tension, stress, and strain.

I live an audacious and spiritually awakened life of abundant wisdom and creativity, love and compassion, peace and joy, as well as of inspirational service to others.

Today, I expect new and interesting things to happen that will open the way to success. I put my whole self into everything I do and pour myself out as a blessing wherever I go.

Thank you, God.

And here's one last Purpose Prayer from Susan Wulfekuhler of Eugene, Oregon. Her life purpose is to celebrate the sacred, create, love, listen deeply, gather threads of meaning, care compassionately, and live bodaciously.

Holy One,

In this new day, I pray:

To live deeply, with purpose,

To celebrate the sacredness of life in everything I do,

To show up in each moment of this day,

To live freely, without attachment to outcome,

To listen deeply to your Spirit within me, to the Earth, to my companions on the journey,

To gather threads of meaning,

To follow my creative dreams,

To care compassionately, starting with myself,

To love generously with my whole heart,

To find ways to be an expression of love and compassion in the world,

And to live gratefully with a generosity of spirit.

Help me to hold this vision and to renew it daily in my heart,

Becoming ever more one with you, my Truest Self.

As you will see in the exercise on creating powerful Purpose Practices, a key component of the exercise is to really get into it with gusto. That doesn't mean you need to shout it from the rooftops, although you could. It does mean that you want to put feeling into it. Creating your Life on Purpose incorporates your mind and your heart—your thinking and your feeling natures. Much of the creative energy will come from your feeling nature, as stated by the Law of Purposeful Creating.

Creating Powerful Purpose Practices

Purpose Practices: Activities in which you engage on a regular basis to keep yourself present and aware of your life purpose.

Looking at the definition above will give us a guideline for creating a powerful Purpose Practice. There are four parts:

1. **Activity**—A Purpose Practice is active. It is something you do.

2. **Regularity**—A Purpose Practice is something you do on a regular basis and over time. If you only do it once, or only once in a while, it is far less effective.

3. **Presence and awareness**—It is only a Purpose Practice if it helps you to stay aware and conscious. Otherwise, it is only a habit.

4. **Life purpose**—Conscious and aware of what? Your life purpose of course!

Here are some guidelines for developing an effective Purpose Practice:

1. **Start with only one practice.** Do that one practice "religiously," meaning each and every day. Try not to miss any days. It is far more effective to do one practice with full integrity than to have half a dozen different practices that you only do from time to time. Start with one.

2. **Fit it into your routine.** Since you want the practice to be something that you can easily do each and every day, be sure you pick something that will fit into your daily routine. For example, my number one Purpose Practice is to walk each morning. While walking I create whom I will be that day by speaking my Purpose Prayer out loud. My Purpose Prayer is my declaration that I will have my Created Life Purpose shape my life for that day.

I use my morning walk as my Purpose Practice for the following reasons:

- I love to walk. Most mornings I walk with my dog, so we are both getting some much-needed exercise.

- I live in a beautiful natural setting where it is particularly relaxing and inspiring to walk, making it that much easier to keep doing my practice.

- It doesn't require a lot of effort to keep this up, even when I am not at home. I could have chosen as my morning practice to get in my car and drive to Jump Off Rock—a truly wonderful place for such a practice—but I know it is unlikely that I'll invest the twenty to thirty minutes to drive up and back each and every day. So, I reserve Jump Off Rock as a secondary practice that I do less frequently (see Purpose Place in a later chapter).

Start with a primary practice that you can easily fit into your routine.

3. **The more active, the better (within reason).** Thinking about your life purpose is less active—and therefore less effective—than either saying it out loud or writing it down. You want your practice to be active enough that it is easy for you to really get in touch with your life purpose. I notice that on the days I really get into creating my Purpose Prayer powerfully, I am more in touch with my life purpose for the rest of the day.

4. **Remember, it is about your life purpose.** Meditating in the classical sense of the word isn't really a Purpose Practice, although it can be a powerful way to prepare for your practice. Classical meditation is about getting in touch with the nothingness of your mind. But that would not be about your life purpose. However, meditating for a while prior to doing your Purpose Practice in some other way, like journaling or singing it, can be a very effective combination.

5. **Have fun.** The more fun it is, the more likely you are to do it. That is, unless you are simply into suffering through life all the time. Remember my client who loves to run and, while he is running, creates his Life Purpose Statement for that day. Keep it light and fun.

Call to Action Assignment: Create a Purpose Practice and start doing it each day for the next twenty-eight days.

You may want to start by making a list of four to five different Purpose Practices you could do and then pick from the list, or mold a few of the items on your list into a trial Purpose Practice. This will be the practice that you will try out for the next twenty-eight days. You can always retire a purpose practice if it doesn't continue to help keep your life purpose in your awareness. Just be sure you create another one to take its place.

I also recommend that you let several people around you know what you are doing. Starting a new routine can be a real challenge for many people. You do it for a few days, then life takes over and before you know it, the new routine is out the window—and with it, so is your life purpose. Do not let that happen. Engage other people in helping to support you in this important tool for living true to your purpose.

Bonus Assignment: Create one or more Purpose Ponderings to use for the next twenty-eight days to help you keep your Created Life Purpose alive and well in your awareness.

THE PURPOSEFUL PIVOT

The Purposeful Pivot is like most of the Tools for Living on Purpose—amazingly simple to understand and well worth investing time to master. The Purposeful Pivot can serve not only as a truing mechanism that will alert you when you are off purpose and allowing your Inherited Purpose to shape your life, but it can also serve as a means for putting yourself back on course. And the more you work with Purposeful Pivoting, the more proficient you will become and the better able you will be to stay true to your life purpose.

To further understand how Purposeful Pivoting works, we can compare it to the autopilot in a plane. Let us say you want to fly from New York to Los Angeles, but as the pilot you do not want to stay at the controls the whole time. You might elect to use the autopilot to keep you on course. But the truth of the matter is that planes on autopilot are off course most of the time. The autopilot in a plane works by making regular, small adjustments. If the plane starts to veer a little too far south, the autopilot adjusts for a more northerly course. But it is not long before the plane then veers a little off course in the northerly direction; so once again the autopilot adjusts, this time to the south. While the plane may spend most of the time slightly off course, either a little too far north or south, it still ends up at its final destination "right on course."

Purposeful Pivoting works in much the same way. You start your day with an intention to stay on purpose; but, if you're like most people, it probably won't be long before something happens that bumps you "off purpose." Perhaps you oversleep, or you walk into the kitchen to find your dog has been enjoying a midnight picnic from the trash can and failed to clean up, or you have a fight with your spouse, or get caught up in traffic. For sure, the world gives us all plenty of opportunities to practice Purposeful Pivoting.

You notice that your purposefulness, passion, and playfulness are diminished. Depending on the sensitivity of your autopilot, you may wander off course for quite a while before you realize you are heading in the wrong direction. During this time of drifting off course, your life is being shaped not by your true purpose, but by your the Inherited Purpose.

The moment you notice that you're off purpose you can initiate a Purposeful Pivot. The possibility of Purposeful Pivoting begins in that moment of awareness, which is one way to turn your Inherited Purpose into an ally. Your Inherited Purpose is your ally because it sounds an alert when you drift off course. As you will see in the following exercises, Purposeful Pivoting can be divided into two stages:

Stage One: Detecting the Symptoms of Inherited Purpositis

The idea behind this exercise is to be able to detect when the Inherited Purpose is running the show.

Think of your Inherited Purpose as a viral disease, like the flu. You know when you have the flu because of certain symptoms, such as an achy feeling, fever, coughing, loss of appetite, and so on. You can also tell when you are in good health because there are other symptoms or signs, like feeling energetic, thinking clearly, and having a good appetite. Just like being sick and being well have certain identifying signs, your Inherited Purpose and life purpose have different signs, as well.

Before we move to the second stage of the Purposeful Pivot, let's define the symptoms of your Inherited Purpose with the following four steps.

1. **Identify your Inherited Purpose** and begin to notice when it is operating in your life.

2. **Notice what triggers your Inherited Purpose into shaping your life.** What will set it off? Look at the times when you are faced with a real or apparent threat—what is likely to threaten you or to make you fearful? A letter from the IRS, bouncing a check at the bank, a new home project that will cost a lot of money?

3. **When these things happen how do you react, what are your thoughts?** Notice both the general flavor of your thoughts and any specific thoughts you can recognize. What actions or inactions do you notice? Do you worry about where the money is coming from, find yourself unable to sleep at night, feel like the weight of the world is on your shoulders, feel overwhelmed or like you have to work that much harder?

4. **Allow yourself to get in touch with what you are feeling** when under the influence of your Inherited Purpose. Do not make the feelings wrong, or yourself wrong for feeling them. Most importantly, do not fall into the trap of indulging yourself. Just recognize how it feels when your Inherited Purpose is shaping your life. Do you feel frustrated, harried, rushed? Do you feel sad and sometimes angry?

What you distinguish in steps three and four are the symptoms of your Inherited Purpose running wild.

Debriefing the Exercise

Why is it important to identify the symptoms of your Inherited Purpose? Because once you do, you can use them to detect when the Inherited Purpose is beginning to operate. The earlier you identify the symptoms, the faster you can pivot from your Inherited Purpose to your Created Life Purpose.

To expand upon the disease analogy, as you become more aware of your body and your physical condition, you can often detect a cold or the flu early enough to head it off at the pass. When you start detecting your Inherited Purpose early you can head it off at the pass, too.

If you feel a cold or the flu coming on you can get extra rest, take vitamin C, and so on. When you feel the Inherited Purpose coming on you can implement a Purposeful Pivot, which is the second part of this exercise.

Stage Two: Making a Purposeful Pivot from Your Inherited Purpose to Your Created Life Purpose

The first stage of making a Purposeful Pivot is to thoroughly distinguish when your Inherited Purpose is shaping your life and then making a conscious choice. You may either choose to let your Inherited Purpose continue to run the show, or you can choose to have your Created Life Purpose shape your life.

The Purposeful Pivot actually becomes possible as soon as you distinguish what is presently shaping your life. You do not need to indulge yourself, just notice what's present. By becoming aware of your Inherited Purpose, you are bringing it from the background, where it has the most power, to the foreground, where it loses its grip on your life.

But identifying the Inherited Purpose is not enough. Oftentimes when someone first starts working with this distinction they become very good at noticing it shaping their life. Sometimes it looks like it is shaping everything. But then they allow it to continue to run. In effect, they're choosing the default mechanism by default—by not consciously choosing something else.

Here's where the Universal Laws of Attraction and Purposeful Creating comes into play in making a Purposeful Pivot. Remember, the Law of Attraction simply stated is: "Like attracts like." Let us map this law onto the distinctions of Inherited Purpose and Created Life Purpose. Your Inherited Purpose is made up of past-based beliefs that appear real or true because you have been living as though they were true for so long. These beliefs are composed of life-distracting thoughts and feelings, and these thoughts and feelings attract similar thoughts and feelings to themselves. With each Inherited Purpose thought, the feelings of disempowerment increase.

In other words, the Law of Attraction works to attract what you do not want as much as it works to attract what you do want. The Universe is nonjudgmental in this way. So if you want to experience a life shaped by your Created Life Purpose, you need to pivot to Created Life Purpose thoughts and feelings.

When you realize that you are in an Inherited Purpose downward spiral, you know that these thoughts and feelings are attracting more of themselves; so, reverse the spiral by creating thoughts and feelings that are based in your Created Life Purpose.

Important Point: Remember to use the Law of Purposeful Creating to supercharge the attractive nature of your thoughts with positive, purposeful, and passionate emotions.

Making the Pivot

Start by creating thoughts that are consistent with your Created Life Purpose. Think and say your Life Purpose Statement, then add positive, purposeful, and passionate emotion to it. As you continue to do so, you will begin to attract more of the same to you. The more you allow yourself to really get into it, the more powerful the results will be.

If you have difficulty jumpstarting the Purposeful Pivot, go to the source of the thoughts you want to create. The source of Created Life Purpose thoughts is Universal Love, your relationship to God or a higher power, or your spiritual nature. Some ways of accessing this powerful emotion is to envision or look at a picture of someone whom you love deeply, or if possible, go spend some time with the person. I sometimes think that this is why my daughter, Amber, is in my life. Thinking of and being with her make it easier for me to Purposefully Pivot.

Continue to add positive emotions by thinking of times when those emotions were present. Since you want emotions such as love, happiness, and joy, think of times when you were most loved and loving, happiest, and filled with joy. Bring those emotions to the present moment to supercharge your Created Life Purpose thoughts.

Additional Ways to Jumpstart a Purposeful Pivot

- Take a walk in nature, counting the number of things you see, hear, and feel that make you feel good.

- Go spend time with people you care about and who care about you.

- Spend time being of service to someone else.

- Laugh for no reason. Start with a giggle and slowly build up to a rip-roaring belly laugh.

- Spend time with a pet.

- Take good care of yourself. Treat yourself to a bubble bath or an afternoon matinee (comedy or inspirational movies—not melodrama, horror, or violence).

- Count your blessings either verbally or in writing. Do not stop counting until you feel really grateful for being alive.

- Mentally revisit one or more special occasions when you were most present to the miracle and joy of being alive. This could be the birth of a child, a time you made a real difference with someone, a most enjoyable vacation, or so forth.

- Take a trip to your special Purpose Place, where you can more easily restore yourself to your true life purpose.

- Go play with a child or children. Continue to play until you are fully restored.

Viveca Stone, from the Richmond area of Virginia, likes to use a few key phrases to start the pivoting process. "One of my favorites is saying 'I can't wait to see what good comes out of this,'" says Viveca. "Say I am stuck in traffic and running way late—out of control late—for an appointment or I've just received an unexpected bill or speeding ticket. When I stop and say *'I can't wait to see what good comes out of this,'* my vibration lightens, my mood pivots, and I am back in my power and peace of mind. I also then have this expectation of something great happening, and often it does!"

Another pivotal phrase for Viveca is "I cast this burden of lack of (money, time, peace of mind...) on the Christ within and I go free to live in peace, prosperity, and joy." (Slightly modified from Florence Scovel Shinn.)

"This statement is a reminder to me that I have support," says Viveca. "Part of my Inherited Purpose is that I have to do everything myself, and that I can't trust others. This phrase brings me back into the flow and support of my community with spirit, and it feels so good to let go of what I can't control."

Call to Action Assignment: This week, begin to use the tool of Purposeful Pivoting to enhance your life. Notice at least three instances when your Inherited Purpose is shaping your life and use these occasions to practice pivoting. At the end of the week, take a few minutes to journal about the experience. Practice pivoting deeply and with velocity, moving beyond fear, lack, and struggle to a life shaped by Universal Love, abundance, and flow.

PURPOSE PRINCIPLES

Purpose Principles are rules or codes of conduct that are consistent with your true purpose in life.

Next, let us look at how Purpose Principles can also be used to help you shape and mold your Life on Purpose. One way to think of a Purpose Principle is that it is where you come from as you go about living true to your life purpose.

Perhaps the best way to distinguish a Purpose Principle is by an example. Let's pick a Purpose Principle from the list at the end of this chapter, The Twenty-Eight Attraction Principles for Living on Purpose. The Twenty-Eight Attraction Principles were originally articulated in Attraction Coaching 100 by Thomas Leonard, who then made them available to the world of personal coaching to be reframed, as I have done by placing them in the context of living on purpose.

Here's one of my favorite Attraction Principles for Living on Purpose:

Add Value Just for the Joy of It

You can add value for the joy of it, as a natural expression of your life purpose. Unhooked from the need to survive, we are naturally self-expressed.

Pause for a moment and imagine with me what our world would be like if we all followed this principle, going around each day adding value to life and to other people for the pure joy of it. Can you see how this one principle could transform your life and those around you?

Of course, powerful Purpose Principles like this one can also punch the "on button" of your Inherited Purpose. "What do you mean add value for the pure joy of it? Why, I'd starve if I didn't get paid for the value I provide to my customers. Sounds like a good way to put myself purposefully in the poor house."

In fact, one of the signs that you have created a powerful Purpose Principle is if it punches your Inherited Purpose buttons.

Another way to think of a Purpose Principle is that it is a mini-context for your life, another powerful molding tool for living on purpose. They can also be used to focus on particular portions of your life purpose. For example, let's say I want to bring more of an experience of living a life of purposeful, passionate, and playful service to my daily routine. I might work with the principle above, or I might create a Purpose Principle that would serve to guide me in living such a life.

It could be something like this:

I express my life purpose in service to others, with a passionate and playful spirit.

Another fun way to work with the Twenty-Eight Attraction Principles for Living on Purpose is to print them out then cut them into individual pieces of paper—one principle per piece. Then pick one that particularly resonates with you and live from it for the next week. I often do this by taping the Principle of the Week on my computer. It is amazing how often my gaze will fall on the Attraction Principle at just the right moment when I am working with a client, and I end up including it in the coaching session.

The main idea is to have fun with the principles, as they gently shape your actions to be consistent with your life, and in so doing, help you to polish your Life on Purpose.

Call to Action Assignment: Pick an Attraction Principle from the following pages, either at random or by selecting one that you feel would be particularly powerful and fun to engage in for the next week. Keep a copy of it with you to help keep it in your awareness. See how many times during the week you can apply it to your life. At the end of each day, journal on what insights you've gleaned from the principle.

Continue this process for four to six weeks or longer if you find it a powerful support structure for living on purpose.

The Twenty-Eight
Attraction Principles for Living on Purpose

1. Become Incredibly Selfish.

Spend your days with "in the beam" activities—those activities that are full expressions of your life purpose—and delegate "out of the beam" activities to other people who will find those activities to be "in their beam."

2. Unhook Yourself from the Future.

Have your life purpose shape your life today. Do not relate to it as a "someday phenomenon." Express your life purpose today; do not wait until you have your act together.

3. Over-Respond to Every Event.

In each situation, express your life purpose fully. Do not hold back. To "over respond" means to come fully from your Created Life Purpose. Reacting is a product of an Inherited Purpose.

4. Build a Super Reserve in Every Area.

It is difficult to completely give your life over to the expression of your life purpose if your basic needs aren't being met. Lessen the pull of your Inherited Purpose by building up super reserves. Here are some of the things you want more than enough of: love, companionship, quiet time/ solitude, money, purposeful projects, energy, and health.

5. Add Value Just for the Joy of It.

Value for the joy of it comes from the natural expression of your life purpose. Unhooked from the need to survive, we are naturally self-expressed.

6. Affect Others Profoundly.

The more you touch others, the more attractive you are. When you express your life purpose you naturally touch and affect others.

7. Market Your Talents Shamelessly.

Your talents are the gifts given to you by God so that you can fully express your life purpose. Marketing God's gifts is attractive and allows you to play full-out in expressing your life purpose.

8. Become Irresistibly Attractive to Yourself.

Living true to your life purpose requires that you become increasingly attractive to yourself. When you find yourself attractive, others will too.

9. Get a Fulfilling Life, Not Just an Impressive Lifestyle.

A fulfilling life comes from...you guessed it, knowing your life purpose and living true to it. Great lifestyles are fine and can be a lot of fun as long as they do not interfere with your life purpose. They also become less important.

10. Deliver Twice What You Promise.

There are two parts to this: First, quit promising the moon. Over-promising is a product of self-doubt and ego. When you know who you are and have the experience of living true to yourself daily, over-promising isn't necessary. Second, delivering twice what people expect is fairly easy when you are expressing your purpose naturally.

11. Create a Vacuum That Pulls You Forward.

Create games and Purpose Projects that are larger than you are, or than you think you are, then let the vacuum such a project creates call you to be that new person.

12. Eliminate Delay.

Why would you want to delay expressing your purpose? It is like waiting to live. The more your life is a full expression of your purpose, the more reason you have to eliminate delay in expressing yourself.

13. Get Your Personal Needs Met, Once and for All.

This is related to building a super reserve. Unmet needs attract others with the same unmet needs. Many needs are based in the survival mode of your Inherited Purpose. Identifying these needs is the first step to handling them once and for all. The more of them you handle, the more room you have in which to express your life purpose.

14. Thrive on the Details.

In the context of life purpose, the details to thrive on are the moment-by-moment expression of your life purpose. Thriving comes from the awareness of the moment and being grateful for each moment. "God is in the details." You may never get all the details right, but when you realize that a life lived on purpose comes from each moment, it is a lot more fun to play with details.

15. Tolerate Nothing.

That is, nothing that's inconsistent with living a Life on Purpose. To do this, you must first identify what you are currently tolerating, and then systemically eliminate each of those things one by one.

16. Show Others How to Please You.

People are pleased when they are living their life purpose, so showing others how to please you starts with sharing with them who you are and what you are up to. Then, it is a natural step to let them in on what they can do to help you express that purpose.

17. Endorse Your Worst Weaknesses.

This means to fully embrace your Inherited Purpose as an integral part of who you are. Remember, you're not trying to get rid of your Inherited Purpose. As far as we know, it will not go away anyway, so just embrace it. Embracing your Inherited Purpose helps to further distinguish it, bringing it from the background to the foreground of your life. Owning your Inherited Purpose allows you to share it authentically with others, which even makes it possible to have your Inherited Purpose forward your true purpose.

18. Sensitize Yourself.

The more in touch you are with your purpose, the more awake you become to life and to the rich bounty of resources all around, just waiting to be utilized for the expression of your life purpose.

19. Perfect Your Environment.

Your environment is an important facet of what calls you to be. It is either calling you to be your Inherited Purpose or your true purpose. An integral part of your environment is the people in your life. Surround yourself with people who know you as your purpose and who endorse and support your expressing it fully.

20. Develop More Character Than You Need.

See the movie Les Miserables for a demonstration of character. Jean Valjean takes living a life of integrity to the next level—the level of character.

21. See How Perfect the Present Really Is.

Those moments when it looks like the present isn't perfect are rich with opportunities and unrecognized resources. In a "there-are-no-accidents" universe it is our job to recognize the perfection of those imperfect moments.

22. Become Unconditionally Constructive.

A life purpose based in possibility, with no need to fix anything, makes it easy to be unconditionally constructive.

23. Orient Exclusively Around Your Values.

Since values are an integral part of your purpose, orienting yourself around your purpose works as well. You can start by making a list of activities that are fully "in the beam" of your life purpose, and a second list of activities "out of the beam," or which are not full expressions of your purpose. Then fill your life with "in the beam" activities and delegate the rest to others who will find those activities in the beam for their purpose.

24. Simplify Everything.

Two natural byproducts of knowing and living your life purpose are focus and simplicity. Keep whatever is needed to help you live your purpose, and get rid of everything else.

25. Master Your Craft.

Be the best at the God-given skills and talents that allow you to fully express your life purpose.

26. Recognize and Tell the Truth.

Develop the skill to be able to tell the truth in a way that it can be heard. Orienting yourself around telling the truth allows others to get in touch with their own truth and purpose, and it is a great way to express your own.

27. Have a Vision.

A life purpose that expands beyond you is really a vision for the world.

28. Be More Human.

When you are genuine, you are attractive. When you are expressing your life purpose, you are genuine.

*These principles are based on the Attraction Principles articulated by Thomas Leonard, www.attractionu.com. Adaptation by W. Bradford Swift, founder of Life on Purpose Institute, Inc.

PURPOSE PROJECTS,
PURPOSEFUL PLAY, PATIENCE, AND PERSISTENCE

Up to this point, the Power Tools for Living on Purpose have focused on expanding your level of consciousness and awareness by defining who you are and what your life purpose is. But as you will recall, though your life purpose lives in your consciousness and awareness, that is not the only place it needs to live to really flourish. It also must live in the consciousness of other people.

In other words, for you to live your Life on Purpose most powerfully, the people around you need to know and relate to you as your true or Created Life Purpose. A Purpose Project is one of the most powerfully effective ways to bridge this gap in consciousness.

Remember, the Purposeful Problem you have created for yourself is that even though you have clarified your Created Life Purpose, the people around you are still relating to you as your Inherited Purpose because you have trained them to do so. Now, it is time to begin to shift how they relate to you, and Purpose Projects are key in assisting them in making this shift.

Purpose Projects are unlike any other type of project you may have worked with in the past. Some people love projects, while other people hate them. I have found in my years of coaching that some people— including myself— have some pretty smelly "baggage" or disempowering history when it comes to projects.

One of my earliest memories of projects was the first science project I had to do in the fifth grade. While the teacher gave us several weeks to work on the project, I, like a typical fifth grader, waited until the night before it had to be turned in to start it. My project was to create a replica of an active volcano that was to be made out of papier-mâché. My mom and I ended up staying up most of the night to complete it. Obviously, my mother was far from pleased with me and I heard about my tendency to procrastinate for days.

So, whatever your history with projects, just know that Purpose Projects are different. A Purpose Project must meet the same four criteria as your Created Life Purpose. Let us look at these criteria and how they shape and form a Purpose Project.

1. It is Satisfying and Fulfilling, A Life of No Regrets.

If your Created Life Purpose gives you a satisfying and fulfilling life and a Purpose Project is an expression of your life purpose, it stands to reason that Purpose Projects will be satisfying and fulfilling. On the other hand, if it is not satisfying and fulfilling, it is not a Purpose Project — no matter how worthy it might seem. For example, one of my clients created as her first Purpose Project to clean her house from top to bottom. Apparently up to that time, she had been a mediocre housekeeper and felt this was an important step to living on purpose. It probably was, but it just was not a Purpose Project. Why? In the process of cleaning her house, she was not experiencing living true to her purpose. It was something she felt she had to do so she could begin to live on purpose. In other words, there was no real connection between the project and her purpose. It is important that your Purpose Projects arise from and are an expression of your life purpose. Remember, the primary point to a Purpose Project is that you are able to live, express, and be known as your life purpose during the time you are at work on the project, not just at its conclusion. We will learn more about this when we distinguish Purposeful Play.

2. A Life Purpose Being Expressed is Inclusive — It is in Service to Others.

When you map this onto your Purpose Projects, it means your projects need to involve other people — and the more the merrier. Your Purpose Project will be a reflection of you expressing your life purpose while being of service in some way. Let us look at another example to illustrate this important point.

My first Purpose Project was, ironically enough, entitled Project Purpose. At the time, one of my primary activities was writing for national magazines. However, most of my writing was more a reflection of my previous career as a veterinarian, and not a clear expression of my life purpose, as I wanted. So, in an effort to bring more of my purpose to my writing, I created "Project Purpose: To write and publish articles about people and institutions whose lives and missions are part of a bold and inspired purpose or vision."

Once I created this project, I began to attract some perfect subjects for these types of stories; so, it was not long before I was sending out queries to magazines proposing Project Purpose Profiles. One of my objectives in this project, besides bringing more purpose to my writing, was to inspire people to live more purposeful and passionate lives. I figured that if they read an inspirational story about some of these "unsung heroes," they might see how they could contribute to their own communities.

Within a couple of months, I had my first assignment to write a feature article on Bo Lozoff and the Human Kindness Foundation for New Age Journal. It was an assignment made in heaven. I had met Bo at a spiritual retreat in Black Mountain, North Carolina, a few months before and had been impressed by his message and his mission to bring more spirituality to prisoners. Now, with the assignment, I was privileged to spend time with Bo and his wife, Sita, at their foundation—and I was getting paid for it.

At the same time, I was beginning to notice that people were relating to me not from my previous profession as a vet, but as my Created Life Purpose. At the end of the assignment, New Age also paid me twice as much as I had ever made on a single article. I knew I was on to something.

As I continued writing Project Purpose Profiles, it was not long before most of the other writers and editors that knew me were relating to me in an entirely different way—as my Created Life Purpose.

What I didn't realize until a year or two later was that there was an added bonus I never would have predicted. One of the main people I inspired into action was myself, because it was from these purposeful interviews that I began to realize that I could create an organization that would be an expression of my Created Life Purpose, just as many of the people I had profiled had done. Thus was born Life on Purpose Institute, Inc. Needless to say, Purpose Projects can be very transformational.

3. A Life Purpose is Based in Love, Not Fear.

Not only does this mean that Purpose Projects should be something you love to do, as we already discussed, but they should also come from love and from possibility. In other words, Purpose Projects are not about fixing something that is wrong, but are instead, about expressing a possibility in life. This is a tricky point, so let us explore a little further.

First, I am not saying there is anything wrong with projects that arise from a perceived need to fix something. Take M.A.D.D.— Mothers Against Drunk Drivers. This organization was started by Candice Lightner, among, others when her thirteen-year-old daughter, Cari, was killed by a drunk driver, without a valid driver's license, who had been released on bail for a hit-and-run drunk driving crash. Candice was out to fix something that she felt was wrong, and has had a very powerful impact on our nation's laws against drunk drivers.

What I am suggesting, though, is that a Purpose Project is not based in a need to fix something, but instead is based on a possibility. Life on Purpose Institute is a "meta" Purpose Project because it is a compilation of many other Purpose Projects. Our mission is to deeply and profoundly touch and contribute to at least 1% of the world's population by assisting people to clarify and live true to their purpose. This mission is based in the possibility of a world on purpose.

However, if I am not careful, it could devolve into trying to fix people that are not clear about their purpose. That is the tricky part of this point. A Purpose Project can start by being based in love and possibility, but it can later devolve into a project based in fear and being positional. It is all a matter of "who you are being" as you work on the project. Of course, as soon as you notice your project coming from fear you can begin to Purposefully Pivot back to love.

Here's another example of a Purpose Project that demonstrates how to move from complaint to possibility. Eric Miller, my client who created the project, describes it best in his own words:

> As part of my Life on Purpose project, I chose a project that would address several concerns and issues. As a parent of a child with Crohn's Disease, I decided to "put my money where my mouth was." I have had a complaint about the treatment of Crohn's, as there is no cure at this point and

the treatment can often have effects worse than the symptoms of the disease. My project was to contribute a portion of my income toward research in finding a cure.

Crohn's is a disease that affects the intestines and can be very debilitating. I figured that if I was able to make a contribution to the research, that would be the start to being proactive instead of complaining about the treatment. In essence, I was a part of the treatment. I committed to donating a portion of each commission check I received in one year. I knew that I was going to have a good year, and thought my donations could make a difference. In fact, I was so committed and fortunate to have such a good year that I ended up donating more than $58,000 to the Crohn's and Colitis Foundation, and partially funded a Research Grant being conducted at the University of North Carolina. The Grant was named in honor of my daughter, Melissa Miller.

In addition, my daughter was chosen that year as the Youth Ambassador of the Carolinas. As a result she wrote an article for the Crohn's and Colitis Foundation–Carolinas Chapter Newsletter. The article was addressed to other teens and children dealing with the disease. The message was a very positive and inspiring plea to live life as if you are special instead of handicapped as a result of the disease. She said that sometimes she feels sorry for herself, but then convinces herself that one of the special things about her is ability to overcome the challenges of Crohn's and that she is a stronger person for it.

This Purpose Project proved to me that one person can do more than they think if they will "step out on the limb" and make a commitment. At the start of the project I pledged $30,000 to the Foundation, yet nearly doubled that number by the end. I believe my real estate sales doubled as a result of this commitment, because it was my life purpose and my love for my daughter that inspired my work. I know the project made a difference, as one doctor was able to conduct a study for two years on the environmental impact on Crohn's patients, and this money helped fund that research.

While my daughter may have this condition for the rest of her life, I will have the memory of not sitting back and complaining that nothing could be done. In this way I have been an integral part of my daughter's treatment so that she, too, could live her life on purpose.

As often happens with Purpose Projects, the results extended far beyond Eric's original expectations.

4. A Life Purpose is the Context and Vessel That Holds and Shapes Your Life — You, in Moments of Time, Doing "Stuff."

There is a bit of a paradox here. On the one hand a Purpose Project serves as a bridge from the domain of being to the "real world" of doing and having. And at the same time, it is important not to forget that your Created Life Purpose, from which your Purpose Project arises, is a matter of who you are, which then gives you "what you do" as an expression of that life purpose.

We will explore this Purposeful Paradox in more depth when we distinguish Purposeful Play later in this chapter.

Creating vs. Recreating a Purpose Project

There are two ways of formulating a Purpose Project — creating from nothing, or recreating an existing goal or project as a Purpose Project. Don't feel like you have to create a whole bunch of new projects in your life. If you already have a full plate of activities, this could send you into overwhelm. Instead, look to see which of the activities in which you are currently engaged could be re-framed as a Purpose Project.

For example, Project Purpose was a recreated Purpose Project. I was already writing and publishing articles for magazines. I even had written one or two profiles that fit the criteria of a Purpose Project-type article. So, I simply re-framed my writing as a Purpose Project. On the other hand, Life on Purpose Institute was created from nothing. Before the Purpose Project there wasn't such a company. It came into being as a result of the Purpose Project.

Next, we will examine a useful structure for creating powerful Purpose Projects, called the Life Purpose Project Page.

LIFE PURPOSE PROJECT PAGE

When you are inspired by some great purpose, some extraordinary project, all of your thoughts break their bonds: Your mind transcends limitations, your consciousness expands in every direction, and you find yourself in a new, great, and wonderful world. Dormant forces, faculties and talents become alive and you discover yourself to be a greater person than you ever dreamed yourself to be.

—Patanjali, Indian philosopher

Life Purpose: Start your Purpose Project Page by stating your Created Life Purpose. As you do so, allow yourself to be present to the greatness, awe, and wonder of the life purpose, and of yourself as you live true to this purpose. This will assist you in maintaining a strong connection between your life purpose and your Purpose Project.

Project Name: Create a catchy, empowering project name that will capture some of the zip and inspiration of your life purpose. If one doesn't come readily to mind, continue on with the Project Page and come back to this later. Oftentimes, the project name will come to you in the process of creating the project.

Project Vision: This next part is vitally important. You are about to take a trip to the future by envisioning how your Purpose Project looks upon completion. Paint a verbal picture of what the project looks like, as well as what it will feel like upon its completion. Imagine that your project took off "beyond your wildest dreams." How has it contributed to your life, to your loved ones, and to the rest of the world? What has your soul experienced as this project was being fulfilled? What have the other people who have been a part of the project experienced? How has it touched their lives? Remember, do not just look to see what it is like at the completion of the project, but also at each step along the way. Make the project real with specifics. How many people have been involved, who are

195

they, what results did you produce, and so on? Remember to step into the future. You are not standing in the present and looking towards the future. You are standing in the future with the project completed and sharing what it is like.

Remember the example of climbing Mount Everest to get a good idea as to why this is so important.

Current Reality: As you continue to stand in the future with the project successfully completed, look back to the current reality regarding this project. Take a few minutes to describe what the current reality looks like to you from the future—from the place where your Purpose Project has been completed beyond your wildest dreams. What does it feel like? What obstacles or roadblocks do you see that you have moved beyond? These could be physical, mental, or emotional roadblocks. Where did your Inherited Purpose come into play to try and stop you in its effort to keep you and it safe, and how did you pivot beyond it? Remember, you are looking back from when the project has been successfully completed. From this perspective, you will be able to see the successful resolution of these apparent obstacles more readily.

Be Prepared to Release: As you grow in your expression of your Created Life Purpose, there will be components of your Inherited Purpose need to be released to make room for the new you. List any fears, limiting beliefs, or lack of consciousness that you are prepared to release to make room for the fulfillment of this project. You can continue to add to this list as you work on the project.

Resources to Attract: What resources will you need to fulfill this project? Of course, more things may come up as you are working on the project, but start now to attract those resources you know you will need by writing them down.

Targets/End Results: A Purpose Project bridges the gap between the visionary aspect of a life purpose and the real world of distance, time, and form. In other words, a Purpose Project has certain results that are measurable, just like each game has a way to keep score. Depending on the size of the project, you may have interim targets or milestones as well as the ultimate result. But it is the result that makes the project real in the physical world. We will look at a special way to relate to this result when we explore the distinction of Purposeful Play.

Write it All Down: Write down the actions that you need to take to move forward on the project, as well as the target completion dates. Add to this area as you move along in the project. Review your Purpose Project Page weekly to keep the purpose and the possibility alive for you.

Contributing and being of service to others is inherent in the expression of your life purpose. It will greatly enhance your experience of living true to your purpose if you are aware of who you are contributing to through this project and how. So, keep a list of people who have benefited from your project, and what contribution was made to their life. You can create a separate page for this area and add to it on a regular basis. Also, by sharing this with your coach, you can keep this important part of the project in existence.

Whenever you feel a bit down or off purpose, pull out this page and read over the difference you have already made. It is sure to boost you back on purpose.

On the next page you will find a blank Purpose Project Page to use as a template for creating your own projects.

Life Purpose Project Page

> *When you are inspired by some great purpose, some extraordinary project, all of your thoughts break their bonds: Your mind transcends limitations, your consciousness expands in every direction, and you find yourself in a new, great, and wonderful world. Dormant forces, faculties and talents become alive and you discover yourself to be a greater person than you ever dreamed yourself to be.*
>
> —Patanjali, Indian philosopher

LIFE PURPOSE:

PROJECT NAME:

PROJECT VISION:

CURRENT REALITY:

WHAT YOU ARE PREPARED TO RELEASE:

RESOURCES TO ATTRACT:

TARGETS/END RESULTS:

NEXT COMMITTED ACTION(S):   DATE:

PEOPLE WHO HAVE BENEFITED FROM THIS PROJECT

PERSON: CONTRIBUTION MADE:

Call to Action Assignment: Create or recreate at least one Purpose Project this week using the Purpose Project Page format. Pick a Project that will enhance your life, that will be fun to engage in, and that will include other people. Select one that might be a bit of a stretch, but not so large as to become overwhelming.

Share the project with two or three people who you know will be supportive.

PURPOSEFUL PLAY

Next, we will learn to use another powerful tool that will assist you in living true to your life purpose. With the tool of Purposeful Play you will find ways of allowing your life to be shaped by your true purpose instead of by your Inherited Purpose, especially in one particularly important place: your relationship with results.

Let's face it, we are nuts about results. What I mean by this is that we make up games, and as part of the rules of the games we determine how we are going to keep score so we know whether we are "winning" or not. Then, oftentimes the game becomes all about the score and we forget that we created the game to express our natural creativity and to have fun. Some of the games we invent under the heading of business, others under the heading of education, and still others under the heading of relationships and marriage. All have certain results we are interested in producing, but I am suggesting that the purpose of these games is really not just about the score or the results.

This is especially true about Purpose Projects. Take a moment and consider this question:

What is the primary purpose of a Purpose Project?

Think about what you have been reading. You can even look back over the pages of this book to see if you can discern the answer, and then write your response below.

_____

_____

_____

_____

The primary purpose of a Purpose Project is for you to be, to express, and to be known as your Created Life Purpose. That is it! Now, to make the game more interesting we often make up some results and outcomes that we intend to produce. But remember, the primary purpose of a Purpose Project is not really about those results at all. Sure, you play the game like it is about producing the results; but all the while you will remember that the real purpose of the project is to be, to express, and to be known as your life purpose. Now, let us look at the definition of Purposeful Play to see how this all ties in together.

Purposeful Play: Working on a project, goal, or task in such a way that you are willing to play and experiment with it while maintaining a particular plan or intention. The secret to Purposeful Play is being committed to a particular result or outcome without being attached to that outcome.

There are three important parts to this tool for Living on Purpose: First, there is the experience, way of being, or attitude that you carry into the project, goal, or task. In Purposeful Play you are ready to experiment, to explore, and to discover. There is a lightness and playfulness to the activity.

Second, as you enter into the project your actions are not random, but are guided by an intention or purpose. After all, the project itself arises from your Created Life Purpose.

Third, the freedom to be playful comes from remaining committed to the project, goal, or task without getting attached to the results. In other words, you remember along the way that the true purpose of the project is for you to be, express, and be known as your Created Life Purpose. While you are committed to producing certain results, you stay free and unattached to them.

This also includes being free to produce other results that you had not expected, as often happens in an experiment. While one of my intended outcomes with the writing project, Project Purpose, was to inspire people into action to live a more meaningful and purposeful life, I had no idea when I started the project that my starting Life on Purpose Institute would be one of the outcomes—but I accept this result with open arms.

Of course, as you begin to work with Purpose Projects, it is likely that at some point you will forget to Purposefully Play with the project, especially if you are not producing the results you had set out to produce in the timeframe you thought you should. When you begin to feel like the activities around a Purpose Project are difficult and full of effort and the spirit of fun and play is missing, that is a clear warning sign that you have forgotten the real purpose of the project and have become attached to the results. In those moments, return to this page and refresh your memory about Purposeful Play. It can make all the difference in the world.

With Purposeful Play you will continue to experience the enlivening quality of living a Life on Purpose. Remember, one of the possibilities of living on purpose is living a life of no regrets. As His Holiness the Dalai Lama once said, "If after trying to save the world, the world is lost... No regrets."

One of the paths to this degree of commitment, freedom, and non-attachment is Purposeful Play.

PURPOSEFUL PATIENCE AND PERSISTENCE: THE UNSTOPPABLE TOOL

One of the top ten benefits of clarifying and living true to your life purpose is being unstoppable. Many people who have used the Life on Purpose Process and Perspective to live a more purposeful life report becoming much more powerful in persevering with the things they want to be, do, and have in their lives. One of the Power Tools for Living on Purpose that can assist you in becoming unstoppable is Purposeful Patience and Persistence.

Purposeful Patience and Persistence: The process of staying on purpose and balancing the realization that bringing a new level of purposeful living into your life takes time, and at the same time staying persistently in action towards the fulfillment of your Purpose Projects.

Let's face it, there will be times in your life where your Purpose Projects won't go exactly as you planned. Unforeseen obstacles and roadblocks are bound to arise to challenge your level of commitment. When this happens, pull this power tool from your toolbox.

But like a pair of scissors, this tool is most effective when the two parts of it are used in combination. Let's see why.

Patience by itself can often be viewed as a pretty passive state of being. Being patient suggests to me the need to simply sit back and wait for something to happen—and indeed, at times this is the perfect "action" to take. However, if you're not mindful, it's easy for your patience to derail you from your overall purpose and intention. This is where persistence comes in as the other half of the scissors. Being persistent will remind you of what you're truly committed to bringing into reality, and it will be there to re-ignite your enthusiasm and passion when it's time to proceed on purpose.

I like the old saying, "No wine before its time." But remember that while the wine is sitting in the fermentation tank, the yeast organisms are busily turning the grape juice into wine. It only looks like nothing is happening! The same is often true with Purpose Projects. Some of them simply need to ferment for a while before the next more active steps can be taken.

There's another part of persistence that then comes into play, which is revealed by its definition: *Persistent—existing for a long or longer than usual time or continuously.*

The key word is "existing." If you want your Purpose Projects to come into being, especially those that will take a fair length of time to be manifested, be sure you create sufficient "existence systems" for them. An existence system is anything that will keep your project or projects in existence. A notebook with your various Purpose Projects is an existence system, as is a regular time in your time planner when you will open the book and review the progress you're making. Such existence systems are an important part of the bridge that connects your dreams (which are in the metaphysical part of the Kosmos) with "reality" (in the physical part of the Kosmos). The stronger the bridge, the easier the journey and the more likely you will be to reach your destination.

I recently spoke with one of my coaching clients, whose "dream machine" was stuck in off. "I live in Flat Rock, North Carolina, which is as small and remote as it sounds," I said. "I coach people in how to be human beings, with the stress on being. It hasn't been an easy road to get to where I am today as a successful coach, speaker, and writer, but I had a dream over ten years ago to make a difference by helping people to clarify and live true to their life purpose. When I started, the dream was about all I had. That and the faith that if I hung onto the dream and continued to live true to my own life purpose, the CEO (Cosmic Enlightened Officer) of my enterprise wouldn't let me down, and God never has."

If you have a dream to make a difference, even if it's off the beaten track of mainstream acceptability, go for it with Purposeful Patience and Perseverance. Follow the breadcrumbs of your passion, and even if you don't know exactly where they are leading you, you will never be disappointed by where you end up. Living in faith can balance the odds even when it appears that you're going against them.

In the next chapter, we will look at some additional power tools that you may want to include in your life to assist you in staying on purpose. They are Life Purpose Coaching, Purpose Partners, Pods, Pow-Wows, and Places. All of them can be viewed as support structures or existence systems to assist you in the process of living on purpose.

A Potpourri of Additional Power Tools: Life Purpose Coach, Purpose Partners, Pods, Pow-Wows, and Places

A favorite approach, commonly known as the "Lone Ranger Syndrome," is used by many people's Inherited Purposes to keep them from living a fully expressed Life on Purpose. It has been my experience that this is just as prevalent in women as in men. In women, it may masquerade under the disguise of being "Super Woman," or "Super Mom," but it is still essentially the Inherited Purpose continuing to shape the person's life.

Including other people in your life and your Created Life Purpose makes the entire process of living on purpose easier. It is also a lot more fun, which is one of the reasons your Purpose Projects should include other people.

In this chapter we will explore three other ways you can include people as part of your support structure for staying on-purpose in your life, and two additional tools to further support you in living true to your purpose. We will examine the value of having a Life Purpose Coach in your corner, as well as how to create a Purpose Pod of other like-minded people, and the benefits of having one or more Purpose Partners in your life. We will also learn the value of a regular maintenance program of Purposeful Pow-Wows, and of having a Purposeful Place to go when you have strayed far from the Purposeful Path.

Put a Life Purpose Coach in Your Corner

> The Michael Jordans of the world all have coaches,
> the sandlot players do not.
>
> — Don Maruska

Don Maruska's quote says it all. By many people's estimate, Michael Jordan was one of the best—if not *the* best—basketball players who have ever lived. Even so, he continued to have coaches throughout his professional life, and continued to listen to them. So, are you interested in being a Michael Jordan, or do you want to just be a sandlot player?

As you will recall from the introduction, I was first introduced to coaching in the mid-eighties, while still practicing veterinary medicine. That coaching relationship was such a positive experience that I've made it a point to have coaches in my life and my business ever since. If you are interested in being an all-star player in your own life, then I strongly recommend having a Life Purpose Coach.

Perhaps reading the Life on Purpose Coaches Creed will give you a deeper understanding of what is possible from a coaching relationship. One way to think of this creed is that it is the stand that we ask our Life on Purpose Coaches to take before they become certified. It's a declaration of who we commit to being, for our clients and for the world.

Life on Purpose Coach's Creed

Imagine a relationship where the total focus is on you, on your life purpose, and on living true to it...

Imagine someone listening, not only to your words, but also to the soul behind them as it expresses its truest desires...

Imagine someone who will be your partner with you as you hold yourself accountable for living true to your life purpose...

Imagine this person being curious about your dreams and aspirations, your vision for the world, and what you are most passionate about in your life—a person who will help you clarify projects that are consistent with your vision, values, and who you truly are, and will help you develop the means to fulfill them...

Imagine a relationship with a person who is sometimes even more committed to what you want in your life than you are...

Imagine in this relationship you could count on this person to absolutely tell you the truth with ruthless compassion—the truth about your many gifts and talents that perhaps you have taken for granted, as well as where they see you are selling out on your true self...

Imagine a relationship that supports you in breaking free from the self-limiting constraints of your past, where now the voice exposing your limitations is recognized for what it is—a voice from the past—and it is your true spirit that is nurtured to shape and form your life, moment by moment, day by day...

Take a moment and imagine *having* such a person in your life. Then, write down at least two or three ways that you could benefit from having such a relationship.

_____

_____

_____

_____

_____

_____

Purpose Partner

A Purpose Partner is someone who knows your life purpose and relates to you as that life purpose. They also know your Inherited Purpose and are willing to give it room, while at the same time assisting you in moving beyond it when needed. While a coach will certainly also be a Purpose Partner, it is a good idea to have at least one other Purpose Partner who is not your coach and who is not expected to coach you in your life. This could be your spouse, a family member, good friend, or business colleague.

Of course, it is even more powerful if you are able to be a Purpose Partner for your partner, which means that person either knows their life purpose or is in the process of clarifying it.

It is also a good idea to create some guidelines for the Purposeful Partnership so that the two of you will be clear about what you can count on and expect from each other. And, while a good friend can make a great purpose partner, it is important to remain aware that you have two distinct relationships: the friendship and the partnership.

Your purpose partner may also be the start of a Purpose Pod.

Purpose Pods

One of the most common complaints or issues I hear from my coaching clients is that they do not have like-minded people around them whom they can use for support in living on purpose. It can be quite challenging to live a life that appears to run at crosscurrents with the flow of our culture. However, a growing number of people are awakening to the realization that our great American Dream of doing more and more to acquire more stuff is really a nightmare.

Perhaps, the most clearly identified groups of people interested in living more meaningful and fulfilling lives have been identi-fied by Paul H. Ray, Ph.D., executive vice president of American LIVES, Inc., a market research and opinion polling firm specializ-ing in surveys based on Lifestyles, Interests, Values, Expectations, and Symbols of Americans. Ray has identified a group, Cultural Creatives, as a subculture of shared values that makes up a quarter of the American population. Cultural Creatives' most important values are: altruism (being of service), voluntary simplicity, idealism, spiritual development, ecological sustainability, concern for mutuality in relationships, and the importance of cultural creativity and activism for a better world. This group is estimated to be made up of over fifty million Americans who share these values, and further studies suggest that at least this many Cultural Creatives live outside the United States.

So, if one out of every four Americans shares these common values, why can't we find them in our neighborhood? Perhaps it is because we do not have a structure or way to alert each other that we exist. Or, at least we didn't until the Internet. In the years of operating Life on Purpose Institute as an online enterprise and community, I have seen that it is possible to attract a sizable Purpose Pod of people who share many of my core values and my vision for what is possible, and who desire to be purposefully of service, to live an abundant and simple live, and to connect with God.

While it may take a bit of effort and some purposeful patience to attract a Purpose Pod of people around you, it is worth it. Why? Because the more you surround yourself with people of like minds and spirits, the easier it becomes for everyone to live true to their life purpose. While it is great to have people in your immediate geographical area to share your life with, you are no longer restricted by geography.

A good starting point is the Life on Purpose Institute web site at www.lifeonpurpose.com, where we are growing a global cybercommunity of purposeful, passionate, and playful people. See the appendix at the end of this book for additional online resources.

Here is a simple yet effective process for creating a Purpose Pod in your area. Create it as a Purpose Project, using the Purpose Project Page. Here are some additional suggestions.

1. Set a date four to six weeks into the future when you intend to have your first Purpose Pod gathering. Determine the day, time, and frequency that will work best for your schedule. This is simply a target date, which can be adjusted as needed.

2. Determine what the intention and focus of the gathering will be in your own words. Then, create the visionary reality of what it will look and feel like once it is formed. Allow yourself to dream about it and really sense what the experience of having such a group will feel like.

3. How many people do you ideally want to start the group, and to what size would you like to see it grow? Do not worry if most of the people you know do not know their life purpose. That is a great place to start, by bringing together a group of people who would be interested in going through the first stage of the Life on Purpose Process. You can use this book as your guide and as a map along the Purposeful Path. Additional copies are always available at the Life on Purpose website!

4. How will you spread the word about the group? Make a list of possible ways. One of the simplest ways to start spreading the word is to make a list of people you know who would be open to hearing about it. Do not worry whether they would want to be a part of the group or not. Just share it with them and ask them if they know of anyone whom they think would like to participate.

5. Remember to keep in Purposeful Play by not getting attached to the results. Instead, stay focused on the fact that through this Purpose Project you are being, expressing, and becoming known as your Created Life Purpose.

6. On the date and time you targeted to have your first meeting, hold it. Do not worry if you are the only person attending. It is a start. Have the meeting with whoever shows up, then schedule the next one. Encourage people to bring at least one friend to the next meeting. Continue to practice purposeful patience and persistence.

Purpose Pow-Wows

A Purpose Pow-Wow is a great way to combine some of the positive attributes of a Purpose Practice and Purposeful Pivoting with the Universal Laws of Attraction and Purposeful Creating.

I recommend conducting a Pow-Wow whenever you have a new Purpose Project that you want to launch, as well as for anything that seems to have lost its juice or for which you feel your enthusiasm waning.

They are also great to do for the pure fun and joy of the experience.

Start by picking a quiet, serene setting that you enjoy and in which you feel good. Take whatever actions are necessary to raise your energy level to one of joy, satisfaction, and fulfillment—even bliss. This could include taking a brisk walk, listening to uplifting music, playing with your pet, or anything else that brings you joy.

Take a moment to become clear about the focus and intention of the Pow-Wow. You may even want to write it down to bring more clarity.

Now, take a few moments to breathe deeply and with each long, slow breath, feel your body relaxing. Continue like this until you feel peaceful and serene, yet alert.

Next, bring your attention to the intention of the Pow-Wow. You might even want to state your intention out loud or in your mind. What do you truly want from this intention? What does it look and feel like upon completion. If it were to really turn out beyond your wildest dreams, what would happen and what would you experience?

Hold onto this vision for several minutes, continuing to create and expand it while at the same time holding the results lightly in your hands as though they were a fragile bird. In this way you release any attachments you may have to the results while still holding the intention of them.

Purposefully Play in this way for several minutes, allowing your spirit to soar. If any thoughts or feelings of a distracting or disempowering nature arise, see them like a hot air balloon rising to the surface of your consciousness, then release them gently to drift away. Focus on your vision for what is possible.

After ten to fifteen minutes, allow yourself to return to the present moment, energized and refreshed, knowing that even now the perfect resources are coming to you for the fulfillment of your intention.

Purposeful Places

From time to time you may find that you have drifted far from your life purpose. Sometimes life knocks you for a loop and you find yourself so far off the Purposeful Path that you may feel lost and alone. When this happens, you may find the regular daily practices, ponderings, and prayers insufficient to restore you to a course true to your purpose. When this happens to me I have a Purposeful Place in reserve. This is a special place that I have designated especially for those occasions when I can't seem to restore myself completely without a little extra effort.

The name of my place is Jump Off Rock. It is in a beautiful mountain setting with amazing views, and on a clear day you can see for hundreds of miles that take in three different states. I find it to be a very nurturing and spiritual place. It even has several walking trials, with winding paths through the mountain laurels and rhododendrons that populate the Blue Ridge Mountains of North Carolina. I find myself going there on some occasions just for the pure joy of it. At the same time, the most special times are when I really need to get closer to God.

I think part of the reason this Purposeful Place is so effective in restoring me to a Life on Purpose is because I have set it up that way. I have made a pledge to myself that if I need to go there to restore myself, I will not leave the mountain until I have accomplished my intention. Luckily, so far I have not had to spend the night at Jump Off Rock. I am usually able to get back in touch with who I really am within an hour or less. By that time I have had a good long talk with God, I have released the fear and self-doubt that may have been shaping my experience of life, and I can enjoy the ride back home.

I encourage you to designate your own Purposeful Place and keep it in reserve for those occasions when you have been knocked off purpose and need some further assistance in restoring yourself.

REPLACING OFF-PURPOSE PATTERNS
WITH ON-PURPOSE PATTERNS

> *Watch your thoughts, they become words.*
> *What your words, they become actions.*
> *Watch your actions, they become habits.*
> *Watch your habits, they become character.*
> *Watch your character, for it becomes your destiny.*
> — Frank Odtlaw

Have you ever stopped to notice how much of your life is habitual in nature? I believe the saying goes, "man is a creature of habit," and if that is true then the patterns that we live will determine the quality of our lives.

As the quote from Frank Odtlaw suggests, our habits and patterns of thought (and emotions, I might add) are integral to who we become, which ultimately shapes our destiny. In this chapter we will explore how to identify off-purpose patterns that are a reflection of the Inherited Purpose, and how to release them for on-purpose patterns that reflect our true life purpose.

Imagine for a moment that the power that is encapsulated in that last sentence—the possibility of taking a habit that does not serve you, does not nurture you or those around you, and substituting a new habit that nourishes and enhances life. Let's look at a simple example. Let's imagine for a moment that you have a habit of smoking cigarettes, and you have come to the realization, as have many people, that it is a habit that does not support who you truly are.

Imagine not only that you stop smoking, but that at the same time you invest the money, time, and other resources that you had been using to smoke to starting a fitness program at the local gym, a new habit that really does serve what you are up to in life. Now imagine taking one old, non-supportive habit each month and substituting a new, life-supportive habit. What would your life be like in twelve months? It would be unrecognizable! This example gives you some idea of the power in this tool for living on purpose. Well, let's get started.

Identifying Your Off-Purpose Patterns

Take a sheet of paper lengthwise and make five columns. Label each column from left to right with these five headings:

- Off-Purpose Pattern
- Connection to Inherited Purpose
- Taking Responsibility for Inherited Purpose Actions
- Creating a New On-Purpose Pattern
- Implementation Action

Now, in the first column start a list of the patterns that you feel are based in fear, lack, or struggling to survive. You may want to work with the Be–Do–Have Model to see if you can identify different off-purpose patterns in each of the three areas of life.

For example, an off-purpose pattern that you identify in the Be aspect of life might be worrying about whether you will be able to pay your bills each month. Another one could be waking up feeling depressed anytime it is cloudy or raining outside. (These happen to be two that I've identified for myself.)

An off-purpose pattern in the Do section might be splurging at the mall whenever you feel stressed out, or isolating yourself whenever you feel like someone is getting too close to you.

On the other hand, you may identify an off-purpose pattern in the Have section as having an overstock of books or new clothes. No wonder you feel overwhelmed trying to take care of all your stuff.

Obviously, as we have learned in previous chapters, there is often a close connection between the *be* patterns, the *do* patterns, and what you end up *having* in your life—in other words, your results. In fact, the most powerful way to conduct this process is by, no matter which area of life you first identify as having the off-purpose pattern, checking to see how it appears in the other two areas as well. For example, I might recognize that I often worry about paying my bills, especially at the beginning of the month. That's occurring in the Be area of life. Then I look to see what actions, or in some cases, what lack of action takes place in the Do area of my life, and what do I end up having as a consequence.

Or I might notice that I have a surplus of books and clothes around my house. That's the "having" aspect of a pattern, but what are the "doing" and "being" components? Well, I buy books and clothes without ever getting rid of the old ones. And why is that? Now, this can be tricky, because we often don't want to tell the truth about the thoughts and emotions or feelings that shape our actions. Perseverance is important here and will pay off in large dividends because it's at the level of our thoughts and feelings that we can effect the most profound changes.

When writing down your off-purpose patterns, be as specific as possible. Don't just write down that you worry, but see if you can identify the patterns of what you worry about. Sure, there may have been times in your life that you have worried about almost everything, but what are the common patterns of your worrying?

Making the Connection

Next, in the second column, identify the source of each pattern. We know that it is based in either fear, a sense of lack, or a need to struggle to survive, but see if you can be more specific—a fear of what, a lack of what, why do you feel you need to struggle? Your column might look something like this:

I smoke even though I know it is not good for me because deep down inside I do not feel I am worthy of being fit and healthy. Besides, my parents smoked for years and it didn't seem to affect them. These are thoughts and points of view that keep the smoking habit in place.

Or...

I worry about paying my bills each month because, according to my Inherited Purpose, there really is not enough money to go around.

The point in making this connection is to realize how your Inherited Purpose shapes your life through these off-purpose patterns.

Taking Responsibility for Actions from Inherited Purpose

Column three is where you begin to take responsibility for the consequences of your Inherited Purpose. Often, when people first learn about the Inherited Purpose, they use it to let themselves off the hook for the effects their Inherited Purpose has on the world. Saying, "Oh, that's just my Inherited Purpose running the show," isn't the most responsible way to use this powerful distinction.

Begin to take a deeper level of responsibility by writing down the effects your Inherited Purpose has had on yourself and others (i.e. the off-purpose pattern). For example, worrying about money and vocalizing those worries might have led to your avoiding dealing with your bills, resulting in bad credit. Having your bookshelves and closets filled to overflowing with books and clothes may have led to a number of arguments with your spouse.

This step isn't intended to send you into your own pity party about what a rotten person you are. However, it often helps to see what the off-purpose pattern has been costing you. The more aware you become of the cost, the more motivated you'll be to replace the off-purpose pattern with a new, on-purpose pattern.

Create a New On-Purpose Pattern

Column four is where the fun really begins, because you have the opportunity to create new patterns that are consistent with your life purpose. Before starting this next step, be sure you are awake and present to your Created Life Purpose. The idea is not to simply write down a pattern that is the opposite of your Inherited Purpose, because that would mean that it is still arising from and being shaped by your Inherited Purpose.

Instead, being informed by the first columns, you will now create a new on-purpose pattern that arises from your Created Life Purpose. In other words, it will arise from and be based in universal unconditional love, a consciousness of abundance, and being in the flow of the Universe.

Take your time and feel free to create several possible on-purpose patterns for each off-purpose pattern. You can then choose which one calls to you most strongly.

Take Action

The last step is vitally important. Look to see how you can begin to integrate the on-purpose pattern into your life as you release the off-purpose pattern. At the same time, you can choose which pattern to begin. Don't overdo it. Start with one set of patterns you want to change and pledge to work with it for at least the next thirty days before moving on to the next set of patterns.

Also, in the action column, make a note of what support structure you feel you will need to be successful in making the change. Support might include sharing your intentions with a loved one, a Purpose Partner, or your coach. You may also want to invite someone else to make these types of changes with you. We are often much better at keeping our commitments when we surround ourselves with others who are involved in the same process.

Getting Bumped off Purpose

If you have ever tried changing old habits and patterns, you already know that it is not always easy to make the changes. From time to time, you may find yourself slipping back to the old, off-purpose pattern or not being consistent with the new, on-purpose pattern.

Relax. It happens to the best of us. The main thing to remember is to not indulge yourself with an Inherited Purpose attack by feeling sorry for yourself or beating yourself up. That would simply mean more of your life being shaped by your Inherited Purpose. Instead, acknowledge the break, forgive yourself, appreciate yourself and the effort you are making, and then recommit to the new pattern. If you stray off purpose consistently, then it is likely that your support structure is insufficient. Look to see how you can fortify it and then take action to put the stronger support in place.

Off-Purpose and On-Purpose Chart Example

Off-Purpose Pattern	Inherited Purpose Connection	Responsible for Actions from Inherited Purpose	On-Purpose Pattern	Implementation Action
Reacting instead of responding.	Fear of history repeating itself; being forearmed against attacks (which indeed are probably not attacks at all, and may not even be about me).	Recognizing the energy of the IP operating and conjuring up assumptions, which in turn bring up thoughts and feelings from the past that have an emotional charge.	Listen. Breathe. Find that space of calmness within, then from that place respond in a loving, caring manner.	Stepping back and looking at the reality of the situation from a more detached place; not allowing myself to be emotionally charged in a situation, but to respond with compassion instead—after taking a breath and listening.
Procrastination	Fear of being "controlled" by any given situation. An "I will get to it when I feel like it" kind of attitude as a means of feeling in control.	Recognizing that I am really not in control when I procrastinate, that I am really just sabotaging *myself*.	Follow through, in spite of my awareness of my resistance, pivoting toward a place of empowerment rather than sabotage.	Moving through my own resistance; pivoting from that resistance into moving forward past the procrastination.

Call to Action Assignment: Make a list this week of your off-purpose patterns. Keep this list for future reference and to add to as you identify additional patterns. Pick one of the off-purpose patterns and begin the replacing process for the next thirty days. Then work on the next one for thirty days.

THE BOOMERS AT PASSAGE #5

Both of the Boomers were excited to learn about some of the key tools for living on purpose, since they realized that shifting from a life predominately shaped by the "shoulds" of their Inherited Purposes to a life shaped by the passion of their true life purpose was not going to be accomplished overnight. Both were ready to address the question, "How do I live true to the life purpose I've now clarified?"

Their initial focus was on the big three Power Tools of Purpose Practices, Purpose Projects, and Purpose Pivoting. Here are a few of their comments:

Barbara:

I was relieved and thankful to learn about the Power Tools for Living on Purpose because I realized, even as I was clarifying my life purpose, that it was going to take something to really start living true to it.

I've found starting my day with a ten-minute Purpose Practice to be a very powerful and nurturing way to start my day. Right now, I get up a little earlier than Bob. I put on the coffee, as I have always done in the past, and then while it's brewing I walk out to the deck with my journal. It's a beautiful journal my kids gave me years ago. I'm only now getting around to writing in it. I start each journal entry by writing down my Life Purpose Statement, and then I read it out loud to myself. It feels like I'm taking a shower as I let the energy of the statement wash over me. I then write down whatever comes to my mind about the previous day and how on or off purpose I was. I also envision what I have planned on this day, and how my life purpose will shape my activities. I then go fix myself a cup of coffee and return to the deck to finish my journaling and to listen to the birds. It's so great to care for myself like this so that I'm more available to care for others in a fun, loving and wise way.

I have also found Purposeful Pivoting to be a valuable tool for keeping me on track. As my coach pointed out, my life has given me ample opportunities to practice pivoting. Even thinking of the unexpected upsets of life as opportunities to practice pivoting is itself a significant pivot.

Bob:

I'm really enjoying recreating my dental practice as a primary Purpose Project. While I realize that it will take some time before I can truly say that my practice is a complete expression of my life purpose of an outrageous life of adventure balanced with thoughtful contemplation and contribution, I find myself more alive and excited about going to work than I have been in years.

I'm also beginning to bring an outrageous life of adventure to my family as well, with a trip planned for the Fall to go rafting down the Colorado River with the kids.

MASTERING THE TOOLS
FOR LIVING ON PURPOSE

THREE DIMENSIONS OF LIVING ON PURPOSE:
THE SPIRAL OF FULFILLMENT

Our focus during this journey along the Purposeful Path has been to assist you in clarifying your Divinely Inspired Life Purpose so you could experience the joy of living true to it. There are at least two other important aspects of a Life on Purpose. You might think of them as different dimensions because, when each one is incorporated into your life, your life becomes richer and achieves much more depth.

Another way to view these other aspects of a purposeful life is to think of them as spiral—what I call a Spiral of Fulfillment. Besides living a purposeful, passionate, and playful life of service, the other two vitally important components of a Life on Purpose are:

- A Life of Mindful Abundance Balanced with Simplicity, and

- A Life of Spiritual Serenity

While an in-depth exploration of these two components is beyond the scope of this book, the synergistic effect of these three dimensions of a purposeful life is too important to not touch upon, at least.

It is easier to write about the relationship of these three aspects of a Life on Purpose as a circular pattern, though in truth the relationship is more like a three-dimensional spiral. The main thing to remember is that as you continue along the Purposeful Path of living a life of purposeful, passionate, and playful service, it won't be long before it becomes useful to also explore what a life of mindful abundance balanced with simplicity can add to the quality of the journey. The same is true of a life of spiritual serenity. Stay on the path long enough and you are bound to incorporate all three dimensions into your life—and boy, what a life it will be! Through this process you will have the opportunity to become masterful in the use of the Power Tools for Living on Purpose.

A Life of Mindful Abundance Balanced with Simplicity

The basic tenet of this distinction is that we live in an infinitely abundant universe and are, in fact, an integral part of this universe—or as Ken Wilber calls it, the Kosmos. This Kosmos extends infinitely in the physical and metaphysical planes, and we have the best seat in the house, right on the cusp between these two aspects, also identified on the Map of the Kosmos as the And Space.

The more awake, aware, and mindful we are of the abundant universe in which we live, the more we can live and express our Created Life Purpose because we know at the core of our being that we have available to us all the resources we need to be and to express this purpose. And all the resources are available for the asking!

At the same time of knowing and experiencing the infinitely abundant universe, we can stay in balance in our lives by continuing to live simply and elegantly. In other words, we do not need to try to complicate life with more stuff than we need just because we know we have access to an infinite supply of resources. For example, we live on a planet with an abundant supply of air to breathe, so we do not need to hoard it. All we need to do is to breathe in when we need some more, and breathe out when it is time to get rid of some carbon dioxide. Knowing and living true to our life purpose helps us to live a simpler life because we are able to use our life purpose to discern what resources we need to utilize at any given time.

A life of mindful abundance balanced with simplicity is far different than the simple life forced upon many people due to a mindset of lack that leads to a life of poverty and destitution. Such a life is shaped by the Inherited Purpose—by fear, lack, and struggle.

In fact, for many people, it is not too long after they have clarified their life purpose and begun living true to it that they begin to bump up against a new aspect of their Inherited Purpose that is often based in their lack consciousness. This is a perfect opportunity to begin creating a new dimension of living on purpose by exploring in depth a life of mindful abundance balanced with simplicity. (For a more in depth investigation of this, visit the Life on Purpose website for the special report entitled *Purposeful Prosperity: Living a Life of Mindful Abundance Balanced with Simplicity.*)

A Life of Spiritual Serenity

In my view it is nearly impossible to live a purposeful, passionate, and playful life of service coupled with a life of mindful abundance and balanced with simplicity without realizing along the way that the Purposeful Path you are on is also an integral part of your spiritual journey—which includes a life of spiritual serenity.

You can heighten the spiritual experience of your journey by consciously including it in your life through various spiritual practices. Of course, there may also be a few additional obstacles and roadblocks to identify and to then release along the way. For example, many of us have unresolved issues related to our past experiences with religions that were designed to control and keep us safe—in other words, religions that were shaped by the collective, fear-based Inherited Purpose of our culture.

Identifying and then releasing these obstacles and roadblocks is a worthy endeavor because with the release comes a renewed sense of peace, tranquility, and connection to Spirit.

As you travel around and around this Spiral of Fulfillment, your life becomes richer, more satisfying, and more fulfilling. Before you know it, you have stepped into a whole new way of being—what is sometimes referred to as being a Visionary World Server.

BEING A VISIONARY WORLD SERVER

As a Person on Purpose, you have within you the seed that may one day grow into your being a servant to the world—when the context of your life is no longer about you. In fact, at that point it stops being just about your family, your close network of friends, your community, or even your country, and it expands to include the whole world and its role in the Universe.

Some people might describe this stage as becoming a world citizen. I suspect that there are many different names. The point is that as you continue along your Purposeful Path, the territory of your impact often expands.

That does not necessarily mean that the entire focus of all world servers is on making a difference with the six to seven billion other people on the planet, at least not directly. Many world servers work from the "think globally, act locally" approach, meaning that while their actions may be at a local or regional level, they continue to stay alert to the global impact those actions have.

Being a Visionary World Server is not about notoriety or fame. Many world servers will never be well known and will instead operate quietly as unsung heroes, while others will become very well known, though it will never be about the fame or fortune for them. The fame and fortune will simply be what comes with the territory of their particular journey. To read about some of the Visionary World Servers who have touched my life, go to the Project Purpose page at the Life on Purpose website.

Read these articles to be inspired—but be careful not to get caught up in comparing yourself to the people who are profiled. We each have our own path.

I thank you for joining me along the path and allowing me to be our coach and guide. If this book has in some way enhanced your life, I encourage you to share it with others, and in this way we will all be creating a world on purpose. While living true to your life purpose isn't always easy, I believe you will find that it is well worth the effort, so I encourage you to purposefully persevere.

Remember also that traveling the Purposeful Path is not really so much about reaching any particular destination as it is about enjoying the journey each and every moment along the way. Living on Purpose is not a "one-day-some-day" phenomenon. It is a moment-by-moment experience. As it says in the Scriptures, "This is the day that God has made. I will rejoice and be glad in it."

THE BOOMERS AT PASSAGE #6
TWO YEARS LATER

Barbara:

I love my life! I love living a joyful, caring life filled to overflowing with outrageous fun, unconditional love, and inspirational wisdom. And yes, it's true: my life purpose has evolved over the past two years, as has my experience of living true to it. It's been wonderful having Bob as one of my primary Purpose Partners, and now that the kids have all clarified their life purposes our family is one happy Purpose Pod. While the kids are all out of the house now, we still make it a point to connect with them on a regular basis and have started our own annual reunion. It was Bob's idea that the rafting trip down the Colorado would be the start of an annual family gathering. Before we even finished rafting we all decided that the next year we'd meet in Bermuda, and this year we'll be spending a week sailing in the Bahamas.

Of course, the greatest gift of living on purpose is the day-by-day, moment-by-moment experience of living true to my core values and what I see possible for life. Oh sure, I still get tripped up from time to time by my Inherited Purpose, but the length of time I'm off purpose has become less and less.

Bob:

Since clarifying my life purpose, I've hired an associate dentist who has worked out very well, freeing me up to spend more time with my family and in my community. As part of my purpose to be a contribution, I've become a Big Brother for a young boy, Frankie. I look forward to our time together each week.

Barbara and I have also started attending a local church and I find it's a great way to connect with other like-minded folks who are interested in living a purposeful life as well as supporting me in living a life of thoughtful contemplation.

Our annual family gatherings are just one of the ways I've brought more adventure to my life. Last year I purchased a kayak and now I'm a regular visitor to some of the great white water rivers in our area. Of course, there are those around me who think I've gone off the deep end—and that's okay, because I realize the water is fine at the deep end as well.

It is very satisfying to live an outrageous life of adventure balanced with thoughtful contemplation and contribution.

I rejoice in life for its own sake. Life is no "brief candle" to me. It is a sort of splendid torch which I've got to hold up for the moment, and I want to make it burn as brightly as possible before handing it on to future generations.

—George Bernard Shaw

ADDITIONAL RESOURCES
FOR TRAVELING
THE PURPOSEFUL PATH

The following resources are intended to provide you with further support as you continue your journey along the Purposeful Path.

Living the Fulfilled Life Foundational Program

Many people find that the process of clarifying and living true to their life purpose can be greatly augmented by the support of others. Living the Fulfilled Life Foundational Program is like traveling the purposeful path with a caravan of other like-minded and spirited people; and since it's offered by teleclasses (classes conducted through telephone conference lines), you can participate in Living the Fulfilled Life from virtually anywhere in the world.

To learn more about this highly effective and economical way to enhance your life, visit the Life on Purpose website.

Life on Purpose Certified Coaches

In the last decade the popularity of personal coaching has grown tremendously, as people discover the immense value of having a coach in their corner. Some of the benefits of having your own coach are:

- *Focus* — Your coach helps you stay focused on what's most important in your life.

- *Clarity*—Your coach can help you move from confusion to clarity.

- *Confidence*—When you see how much your coach believes in you, it helps build your confidence.

- *Support Structure*—Having regular coaching sessions gives you a structure for moving forward in your life.

Life on Purpose Coaches Development Program: Creating a Global Community of the Most Effective and Successful Life Purpose Coaches in the World

Are you ready to make a profound difference in life? Do you long to make a profound and lasting difference with people? Does the idea of assisting people to clarify and live true to their life purpose call to you? Are you a coach searching for a proven, systematic approach to help people along their Purposeful Path? Do you yearn to be a part of a global community of like-minded people connected by a bold vision for transforming themselves and the world?

Then you owe it to yourself to explore becoming a Life on Purpose Certified Coach. The Coaches Development Program arose as a means for Life on Purpose Institute to fulfill its vision and mission:

The Vision: The possibility of all people living purposeful, passionate, and playful lives of service, mindful abundance balanced with simplicity, and spiritual serenity.

The Mission: To deeply and profoundly touch and contribute to at least 1% of the world by assisting people to clarify and live true to their purpose.

Toward that end we are training some of the most effective and successful Life Purpose Coaches in the world. We have attracted a spiritually-based community of people dedicated to transforming the world to a World on Purpose. Are you one of these people? How might you know?

A favorite quote of mine, from Frederick Buechner, will help you answer that question:

"Where your deep gladness meets with the deep hunger of the world, there you will find a further calling."

Would it be your deep gladness to serve people as a Life Purpose Coach? Are you called to assist others in their transformation from the inside out, and at the same time to continue your own personal transformation? If so, you meet the basic requirement for becoming a Life on Purpose Certified Coach.

To learn more, visit the Life on Purpose Institute website.

INSIGHT PAGE

Insights   *Actions*